1

Tips for First-Timers

Willie Miranda

Miranda Real Estate
Clifton Park, New York

For most people, buying a home is the most important financial decision they will ever make. For those who have never bought a home, it's important to understand the steps involved and what can be done to facilitate the process. The purchase process can seem daunting at times, but with the proper knowledge and advice, it can be fun and rewarding.

Why Purchase a Home?

Perhaps the first thing that any first-time home buyer should ask is, "Why purchase a home?" Whether a first-time or fifth-time buyer, the reason remains the same. For decades, home ownership has been considered a terrific investment, one of the few that are more likely to increase than decrease in value. While nothing is guaranteed, trends have shown this to be true. It is important for first-time buyers to be realistic about what they can afford. Spending more than you can afford turns the normally terrific investment into a very risky one.

The Mortgage Pre-Approval

Meeting with a mortgage professional is the first step to setting a realistic goal. Anyone who needs a loan to purchase a home will need to speak with a mortgage lender to obtain a pre-approval prior to looking at any homes. You wouldn't want to fall in love with a home, only to find out later that you can't afford it. A lender will check your credit and determine the loan amount and interest rate you are qualified to receive. Also, many sellers require that buyers wishing to view their home have already undergone the pre-approval process. Just as buyers ought not to look at homes they cannot afford, sellers want to ensure that the people going through their home have the ability to purchase it.

Obtaining lender pre-approval increases your odds of obtaining a mortgage when the right house is found. Mortgage approval is a critical point at which transactions either fall apart or proceed to closing. Having as much of the work done ahead of time will put you on track to successfully purchase a home. Most mortgage professionals provide pre-approval at no cost or obligation to the applicant.

Setting a Realistic Timeline

The American dream of home ownership is attainable by nearly anyone, but it is important for buyers to set realistic goals and timetables for their purchase. The average time to close on a house is usually four to six weeks from the date the contract is accepted. This time is used to perform inspections, have the house appraised, obtain a mortgage, conduct a title search, obtain homeowners insurance, and more.

Since many first-time home buyers are currently renting a house or apartment, they will need to let their landlord know of their plans to move. If the closing date in the purchase contract calls for a middle of the month closing, buyers should pay their rent through the end of the month so they will be able to move slowly and not feel rushed.

Selecting the Right Agent

According to the National Association of Realtors®, there were 1.1 million licensed agents in the US in 2010. With so many agents to choose from, it's a good idea to interview more than one agent to decide which is right for you. Agents who specialize in working with first-time home buyers should be able to answer any question you may have. In fact, a good way to select the right agent would be to gauge how willingly and confidently they answer your questions.

Experience is also important. Selecting an agent who is familiar with the market will help when making an offer or negotiating repairs. If an agent has sold homes in the same neighborhood you are interested in, their first-hand knowledge can prove to be invaluable during negotiations. The home-buying process can sometimes be lengthy, so it's important to find an agent with whom you feel comfortable.

Looking At Homes

Buyers need to be up-front with an agent before viewing homes. First, let your agent know if you want to see a dozen homes in a day, or just a few per day scattered over a longer period of time. Buyers should establish their ideal time frame for moving and let their agent know when it is most convenient to view homes. Since many homes are not vacant, it may be necessary to schedule showings a few days in advance.

Just as a buyer does not want to be rushed into a home, a seller does not want to be rushed out. Another important tip is to get a list of the homes you want to see in advance, and drive by them prior to going out with your agent. Pictures can be deceiving, and it saves everyone time if the buyer is able to eliminate certain homes that do not appeal from the outside. Once inside the home, it is important to be as objective as possible. A buyer should bring a notepad along to list the "pros and cons" associated with each home. This will help you make an informed decision when determining whether to make an offer.

Knowing the Up-Front Costs

Once the right house has been found, buyers need to be aware of the expenses they are likely to incur before closing. The first of these expenses is the earnest money deposit, also called a "good faith deposit." This money is held in escrow until closing. Assuming all other contingencies in the purchase contract are satisfied, the earnest money will be applied toward the amount the buyer brings to closing.

Since a contract to purchase a home is a legal and binding document, failure on the part of the buyer to follow through with the purchase may result in the forfeiture of their earnest money deposit. While the amount of this deposit varies by region and value of the home being purchased, it can be thousands of dollars.

The next cost that a buyer will incur is for the home inspection. Almost all home, pest, well and septic inspectors require payment on the day of the inspection. While a prospective buyer may not be required to perform these inspections, it is highly recommended. A good agent should make their clients aware of these fees and any other costs that are common in their area.

Selecting the Right Attorney

If you live in a state that requires closing attorneys, you should hire an attorney when the right house is found and you've written a contract. Lawyers have a variety of specialties, and it is a good idea to hire an experienced attorney who specializes in real estate.

A good agent should be able to recommend an attorney with whom they have worked in the past. The attorneys are responsible for approving or disapproving the contract, preparing the title, and organizing all the necessary paperwork to be signed by the buyers at closing. If a potentially expensive issue is discovered during inspections, it is the attorney's job to negotiate with the seller's attorney to cover those costs, either as a credit at closing or a renegotiation of the sales price.

In the event the buyer has a legitimate reason to back out of the deal, the attorney will negotiate the release of the earnest money deposit for the buyers. Proper attorney selection is vital to help insure a smooth transaction.

Reaching the Closing Table

Many things must be accomplished for a transaction to reach the closing table. Reaching this phase of the transaction means that inspections have been completed, the application for a mortgage has been accepted, and the title has come back clear of defects. When the documents are signed and the sale is recorded, the exchange of keys is all that needs to take place.

For a homebuyer, this is truly a time to rejoice. While the process may seem lengthy and stressful, making it to the closing table changes the *dream* of home ownership into a reality. Regardless of the economic climate or market conditions, purchasing a home is a great decision. While it is not something to be entered into lightly, the choice to purchase a home should prove to be one of the best investments you will ever make.

ANSWERS
From
EXPERTS
On Buying a Home

Sage Advice from 18 Top-Selling
Real Estate Agents in North America

Aaron Kinn	Adrian Petrila
Amy Coleman	Bob Zachmeier
Bruce Hammer	Chase Horner
Dawn McCurdy	Frank Profeta
Igor Krasnoperov	Joey Trombley
Kimberlee Canducci	Len Wong
Lester Cox	Lynn Horner Baker
Michael Lewis	Paul Rushforth
Warren Flax	Willie Miranda

Out of the Box Books
Tucson, Arizona

ISBN: 978-0-9801855-2-2

Visit the publisher's website at:
www.outoftheboxbooks.com

When it comes to books… think Out of the Box!

Out of the Box Books
P.O. Box 64878
Tucson, AZ 85728

Table of Contents

TABLE OF CONTENTS

INTRODUCTION

This book will assist anyone, whether novice or experienced veteran, to locate, make an offer on, negotiate, and finance a home. The authors have more than 270 years of combined experience and have collectively negotiated more than 30,000 home sales.

We've arranged the topics in the same order that they typically occur in the home buying process, so as you navigate the path to home ownership, use this book to guide you.

Chapters 1-6 - Education on the home-buying process

Chapters 7-9 - Insight on choosing the right real estate agent

Chapters 10-13 - How to structure your offer

Chapters 14-16 - Negotiating tips

Chapters 17-18 - Financing and property tax considerations

Knowledge arms you with a stronger negotiating position and thus; the ability to strike a better deal. This book will empower you to achieve the American dream of home ownership while avoiding many of the mistakes made by home buyers and inexperienced real estate agents.

Enjoy!

About The Author

Willie Miranda

Miranda Real Estate Group
1482 Route 9
Clifton Park, NY 12065

(518) 348-2060

wmiranda@mrgteam.com

www.williemiranda.com

Willie Miranda started his real estate career in 1999. After winning awards at two national real estate franchises, Willie started Miranda Real Estate Group, Inc. in July, 2002, and developed a customer-service oriented team approach and an aggressive marketing plan.

Willie doesn't just hire anyone; he looks for people who share his core value of giving the customer A+ service. He manages 65 agents and 8 staff members in Clifton Park and Rotterdam, NY offices. Miranda Real Estate ranked in the top 10 in total production volume out of 480 brokers in the Capital Region of New York in 2008, 2009, and 2010. Miranda Real Estate received Business Review's "Great Places to Work Award" in 2005, 2006, 2008, 2009, 2010, and 2011.

In 2005, Willie was selected from 25,000 agents across the United States and Canada to receive Craig Proctor's coveted Quantum Leap Award, for having the most exceptional gains in real estate success. In 2006, he received the Business Review's "Forty under 40 Award."

Willie is known as the "Local Area Real Estate Expert," and is frequently featured on local radio shows and local area television news broadcasts, providing up-to-date information for buyers and sellers on the conditions of the current real estate market. He has had his own radio show, Capital Region Real Estate Today, and has branded himself well in the area.

His commitment to providing outstanding service to his clients and agents goes beyond the realm of just "getting the job done." He genuinely cares about his clients and the professional and personal success of every person in his organization. He is friendly and enjoys meeting people and building new relationships. He understands the importance of not only building new relationships, but nurturing them.

Willie has successfully coached over 250 real estate agents and lenders across the country on how to start-up, grow, and bring their businesses to the next level, and he continues to be seen as a leader and mentor by many in the industry.

In addition to Willie's real estate business, he owns and operates the award winning All-State Insurance Agency, also located in Clifton Park. He has owned this company for approximately seventeen years.

Willie's wife Shari has supported him in the growth of both companies for the past eighteen years. They have two daughters with whom he is active in softball and soccer leagues. Willie and his family reside in Clifton Park, NY.

2

From Contract To Closing

Len T. Wong

Len T. Wong & Associates
Calgary, Alberta

ANSWERS FROM EXPERTS ON BUYING A HOME

The key to understanding home buying is to understand the entire process, from contract to closing. For most individuals, a home will represent the largest purchase of their lives, so the importance of understanding this process cannot be overstated. With proper understanding and education about the process, the home-buying experience can be both enjoyable and exciting.

Pre-approval is the first step in this process: it will help to determine your budget, and thus the price range in which you can expect to purchase. To get pre-approval, buyers can either:

1) Use a mortgage *broker* who uses various lending institutions to find the best rate and mortgage plan
2) Use a bank with which you may already have an existing relationship. Banks typically offer only their own loan programs

When dealing with pre-approvals, a formula will be used taking into account the buyer's salary and debt service. This can determine the amount for which the buyer can be approved and qualified. You should analyze the various options provided and determine which works best based on the payment schedule, amortization, once-a-year pay-outs on principle, payment double-ups, and other factors.

Instead of being focused solely on paying down the mortgage, buyers should focus more on living comfortably. The double-ups on mortgage payments or once-a-year principle pay-outs will make up for it.

Determining the down payment is also important—if the buyer has good credit, they may be able to go with a zero down payment. If not, the down payment may be as high as 20% to avoid mortgage insurance charges. The insurance rate depends on the amount of the down payment. A mortgage broker or banker can explain this information in greater detail.

It is also essential to understand the other costs of the process, such as lawyer's fees at closing. Leave room for them in a budget to prevent any unwelcome surprises. A lawyer will charge a base fee for their services and then add extras, called disbursement fees, onto the base fee.

Disbursement fees can vary depending on the number of costs incurred and the type of property being purchased, such as a condominium or a home. Examples include Estoppel certificates for condominiums, the Real Property Report for homes, and others such as mortgage registration, couriers, and more.

Buyers should also plan for moving expenses. Consider whether you will be moving everything yourself, renting a truck, or hiring a moving company. These costs can add up, especially considering that once moved into a new home, you may need to set up utilities such as cable, internet, electricity, heating, and water.

Property taxes must also be considered. They can be set up to be paid monthly or yearly, and the property owner will make pro-rated payments each month. The potential exists for repair costs if you are buying a "fixer-upper" that will require some cosmetic work. Again, the buyer must budget accordingly for these costs to avoid being caught off guard. Once the pre-approval and budgeting for closing costs are finalized, you will be ready to begin the search for your dream home.

Selecting a real estate agent is the next step in the process. The agent should be knowledgeable and experienced but also have a good sense of what you are looking for, have your best interests at heart, and be willing to educate you in the process. As stated earlier, a home will probably be the most expensive purchase of your life, so it is essential that you feel confident and comfortable with the purchase. The first thing for an agent to understand about the buyer is their budget. This should be learned during the pre-approval process.

Next, you must decide on the type of property you wish to purchase. Do you want a condo, a townhouse, an attached or detached home? Do you have parking requirements, such as a garage that is underground or heated? What about location? Do you want to live in a city? If so, what area of that city? What forms of transportation do you anticipate needing?

Experienced real estate agents will set up their buyer online with their VIP Buyer Profile System. This helps match the buyer's needs and criteria with new listings as they appear. This process will educate you and enable you to narrow your selection requirements as you eliminate properties that don't fit your needs and adjust the amount you want to spend. Buyer's expectations often change as they become more educated. This is why starting the pre-approval process early is so important—so you will know your maximum budget.

Buyers should try not to go to their maximum unless they have seen everything in their initial range and know exactly what their dollar can buy. Most likely, the buyer will not want to be moving again anytime soon, so they should understand the payment process and keep an eye on the long term. The old adage of real estate – "buy low, sell high" - is a reasonable goal if the buyer can minimize real estate fees, closing costs, and the purchase price.

When that dream home is finally found, it's time for the buyer to submit an offer. If possible, the buyer should see if their real estate agent can learn from the seller's real estate agent why the property is being sold. While there could be many reasons, the buyer should keep in mind that under the Privacy Act, the seller is under no obligation to disclose this information. However, if the seller shares this information, it can help you determine your initial offering price.

In determining your initial offering price, the buyer should also take into account other homes in the area that are of similar size and quality. The initial offering price is a strategic move and for it to be successful, buyers should determine their maximum purchase price and work backwards. The negotiation process can be very emotional for both for the buyer and seller which makes your real estate agent a helpful guide.

When a counter offer from the seller is received, buyers must determine if that counter offer fits their expectation on price. The thing to remember here is that with reasonable interest rates, a price difference of $5000 might only represent a $20 difference in the monthly payment—a minimal expense considering that the buyer's goal will be to increase the value of the property over the long term.

Deposits are important to the seller, but the amount of the deposit varies by area. Buyers in Calgary typically deposit anywhere from three to five percent of the purchase price in order to demonstrate to the seller, that they have financial strength behind their offer and that they are sincere about purchasing the home.

When making an offer, buyers will usually require that certain conditions are met before the contract they submit becomes a firm deal. While a buyer's concerns should be satisfied, it is important that they not include too many conditions, as this could negatively affect negotiations. The two most common conditions are home inspection and financing.

Home Inspection - When hiring a home inspector, buyers should make sure that they are knowledgeable. Ideally, the home inspector will be known to the buyer's real estate agent. Their rate will vary depending on the size of the property and its amenities. Buyers typically choose one of three options: a standard home inspection to identify potential structural or mechanical problems, a negotiated flat fee dollar amount, or 1% of the purchase price. The last two options take into account the extra work to inspect additional amenities.
Unless the property is brand new, the buyer should expect that the home will need some work, and avoid trying to

"nickel and dime" the seller. In all likelihood, the purchase price will already take the condition of the property into account. As with other parts of the home-buying process, a real estate agent can be a helpful guide.

A home inspector provides a general overview of the home's condition, assessing both its interior and exterior while checking the functionality of all its mechanical systems, such as plumbing, heating, and electrical. The inspector will complete a report for the buyer to review and will make note of any problems they find.

If there are severe problems, then the buyer should negotiate with the seller to hire a professional to fix them. If there are no severe problems, but only minor maintenance issues, then the buyer should opt to correct them after the sale rather than bringing them into the negotiation process.

Financing - Another typical condition for the buyer to request has to do with financing. As mentioned earlier, getting pre-approval is helpful in determining how much the buyer can afford. Once everything has been approved, the bank may arrange to send an appraiser to the property. Once the bank has completed all approvals and approves the appraisal, they will notify the buyer.

When buying a condo, another condition you may need to meet is a review of the condominium documents. These documents include the by-laws, budgets, financials, minutes, and reserve fund study reports. The documents are usually produced by a condo management company to ensure that the condo is in good shape and that no special assessments or budget increases are expected. This helps the buyer become aware of any upcoming issues and make an informed decision.

If the buyer must sell their home before agreeing to buy a new home they will request a condition called "subject to sale." This condition allows the buyer to enter into an agreement with the seller while retaining the right to either buy the home as agreed or step aside if another offer is received and their home has not yet sold. This is referred to as a "first right of refusal." If another offer is received that doesn't require the sale of the buyer's home, the first buyer usually has from eight to twenty-four hours to make a decision on whether to remove the condition and move forward with the sale without selling their home or walk away from the property. This condition is rarely used. Sellers do not like it because the pending offer tends to keep new potential buyers who don't need to sell a home from viewing their property.

Another item in the purchase contract that demands attention is the possession date. The buyer must decide what date works for them and how that date will affect the cost of closing. A prudent buyer will also take into consideration the frequency of their mortgage payments—whether they are bi-weekly, semi-monthly, or monthly. Buyers with a lot of personal belongings may consider trying to close on their home as much as two weeks early to allow extra time to move and minimize stress.

Chattel is movable articles of personal property other than buildings or land. The purchase contract should clearly specify the chattel included or excluded in the sale. Typically, basic appliances such as a refrigerator, stove, hood fan, dishwasher, etc. are included in the sale. Other items that may also be included are window coverings, garage door openers, a vacuum system, and others which may be negotiable. Usually, washers and dryers are <u>not</u> included in home sales, but are included in apartment condos and townhomes.

Once the buyer and seller have agreed on the price and conditions, the ball enters the buyer's side of the court—it is up to the buyer to work toward fulfilling the contract conditions. The inspection condition will be met if the home inspection is clear or repairs are negotiated. With a financing condition, buyers must provide their lender with the necessary information to obtain approval of the buyer's financing condition and any other conditions that were requested in the purchase contract. Your real estate agent will help guide you in this process.

Once all conditions have been satisfied, it's finally time for the buyer to take possession of their dream home. For this buyer, this is the proper time to contact their lawyer or, if they do not have one, use one recommended by their real estate agent. An appointment with the lawyer is usually set up a few weeks before the buyer takes possession of the home to sign all necessary documents including the title transfer and mortgage.

When everything is signed, the buyer should inform their real estate agent, so they can schedule a walk-through on the possession date to ensure that everything is done. This walk-through will show the buyer that the property has remained in the same condition as when it was first seen. Be prepared though – the home may appear stripped-down without furnishings.

Once the seller's lawyer or real estate agent notifies the buyer's real estate agent that all funds and the mortgage have been received, the keys are released and the buyer finally has their dream home.

It is incumbent upon buyers to understand the process of buying a home from start to finish. An experienced and educated real estate agent will be able to guide you through the process and make the experience enjoyable and exciting.

About The Author

Len T. Wong

Len T. Wong and Associates
#20, 2439 – 54th Avenue SW
Calgary, Alberta T3E 1M4

(403) 287-4888

lenwong@calgaryhomesearch.com

www.lenwong.com

Len Wong grew up in the Real Estate Business. His father, Len Wong Senior, was a successful real estate broker in Calgary during the 70's and 80's with extensive hotel and real estate development experience. Upon completing a Hotel Administration degree in Las Vegas, Nevada, Len followed in his father's footsteps by establishing a career in real estate appraisal, hotel and property management, and development. He served on the 1988 Olympic Organizing Committee and was involved in Corporate and International Olympic Housing for the Calgary Olympic Winter Games.

Len started his career as an assistant to one of the top agents in Calgary. During his 20-year association with RE/MAX he was consistently ranked in the Top 100 agents and in the Top 25 in Canada over the past 10 years. Len has received every top award that RE/MAX offers including the prestigious Circle of Legends Award. Len is ranked in the top ten on the Calgary Real Estate Board (5,500 members) for the most listings and units sold during the past 10 years.

After 20 years at RE/MAX, Len established his own business with his partner of 14 years, Laura O'Connell. They've grown from one assistant to five full-time Agent/Associates and 5 full-time Coordinators who are the "glue" of the operation. As one of the most recognized teams in the Calgary real estate market, they have sold more than one billion dollars of real estate. Len has been featured in various real estate magazines and television news programs over the years as the "go-to" real estate agent in the city.

Len credits his father for his experience and background and his wife, Iris for her support of his business goals over the past 25 years. Craig Proctor, a highly respected real estate coach was an instrumental influence as Len's personal mentor. Of the 25,000 agents in North America who Craig has coached, Len was selected to receive the Quantum Leap Award for the most exceptional gains achieved through the aggressive and systematic implementation of Craig's Quantum Leap System.

Len carries the same success to his personal life and is considered one of the top basketball referees in the Calgary area. He enjoys golfing, yoga and travelling. Len is outgoing and enjoys building relationships with the people he meets. His biggest satisfaction and reward in the real estate business is helping individuals, friends, and families make one of the biggest investments of their lives!

3

Establishing Expectations

Lynn Horner Baker

Horner Baker Partners
Marietta, Georgia

"If a man empties his purse into his head, no man can take it away from him. An investment in knowledge always pays the best interest." - Ben Franklin

ANSWERS FROM EXPERTS ON BUYING A HOME

Home ownership has always defined American culture and the American way of life. For many Americans, their goals and dreams, from a very early age, revolve around the desire for financial investment, security and the culture of community and family lifestyle. Such a common goal among the general population leads to literally millions of people purchasing homes. Unfortunately, knowledge about this process is often gained during the experience itself and not beforehand.

The process of purchasing a home, one of the largest investments in a person's lifetime, is frequently a learning experience instead of an educated, well thought-out course of action. The real estate market of this era and for many years to come is a volatile environment, presenting both opportunities and uncertainties that demand knowledge and expert guidance from a variety of professionals in the industry.

Buyers must first take ownership of the buying process before taking ownership of a property. The saying "knowledge is power" is certainly true when purchasing real estate. Two key figures necessary for success are a strong and competent real estate professional and a knowledgeable mortgage lender.

Buying a home should be an exciting time without surprises or glitches along the way, and a buyer making educated and well thought-out decisions can accomplish just that. By establishing a road map and realistic expectations, the process can be made fun, enjoyable, and most importantly, profitable.

CHAPTER 3 – ESTABLISHING EXPECTATIONS

The initial step for buyers, whether a first-time buyer or an experienced buyer, is to grasp the "affordability" factor relative to their current buying power. A myriad of loan products are available that are suitable for individual needs and it's an excellent idea for a buyer to interview several lenders to determine the best product for their goals.

Additionally, the buyer must expect to have available cash to cover the down payment and some of the additional expenses associated with the purchase. An experienced real estate professional may also negotiate to have the seller contribute to the buyer's closing costs. Some specific government loans, for example, often require the seller to assist with the buyer's closing costs. When this arrangement is made a part of the contract, the buyer will typically pay a slightly higher sales price for the seller to agree to an upfront contribution to their closing costs. In essence, some or all of the closing costs are being "rolled into" the purchase price.

Once the finances are in order, the buyer can focus on the process of home selection. Buying a home is based on a progression of choices. A seasoned real estate agent will schedule an appointment to meet with the buyer and, at that time, interview the buyer about the prerequisites of the home purchase. In buying a home, the buyer should be asked a series of questions in order to define their home buying necessities and requirements.

Having a written and itemized list can relieve some of the stress involved with the actual purchase. Additionally, the buyer must recognize the level of compromise that can be endured. For example, a buyer may build a "wish list" that is categorized, such as "A," absolutely must have, "B," nice to have, but not necessary and "C," this would be a bonus.

It's easy to assume that buyers just want to look at a lot of houses, but not just any house will do. Ideally, the buyers should write down specific features that they want in a home, such as the number and location of bedrooms and baths, whether basement or slab, geographic area or school district, neighborhood amenities, lot size, subdivision, age, style, interior and exterior features, construction type, condition (fixer-upper or move-in ready), and other variables.

Buyers should consider whether they are willing to undertake repairs, updating, or cosmetic changes. The buyer should also consider travel distance to work, schools, places of worship, shopping, medical facilities, family members and/or friends, recreation, and other factors unique to their lifestyle.

Next, it's time to begin the selection of potential properties to view that appear close to meeting the buyer's needs and desires. At this point, the real estate agent has interviewed the listing agent of each property to determine if it meets most of the criteria of the buyer, and then called the seller to set up the showing appointment.

The first day spent with the real estate agent can be characterized, somewhat, as a learning experience, because not every home may be perfect, despite the lengthy information gathering and sharing of criteria between buyer and agent.

CHAPTER 3 – ESTABLISHING EXPECTATIONS

The first encounter of matching the inventory of homes with expectations can go in one of two ways. Either the home product will overwhelm the buyer (a good experience) or underwhelm the buyer (a disappointment) in terms of matching their buying criteria. This is where the fantasy of the dream home collides with the reality of what is actually for sale. It's entirely possible that the buyer with a skilled agent will identify their ideal home within the first few showings.

At the end of the day, expect to spend some time with your real estate professional to review the homes you have seen. It's a good idea to establish a benchmark by which all other homes are compared, as well as a second or third choice. When there are subsequent days of viewing homes, it's always a good plan to go back and see one or two of the favorites from the first excursion. This will keep them fresh in the mind of the buyer as a good basis of comparison.

Buyers should have a good feel, by this point, for the size, condition, and extra features of a home for a specific price range. A buyer shops by comparison and, all the while, looks for reasons not to buy a home—this is a process of elimination. Keep in mind that, when one buyer finds a home that they love, other buyers may find it also. Many potential buyers miss out on a home due to inaction.

As the perfect home rises above the rest, the decision is made to write an offer. Your agent will call the listing agent to verify availability, to determine if there are any other anticipated offers being written on the home, and to ask general questions about the timing or special circumstances of the seller that need to be factored into the offer.

This information is used to determine the approach to pricing. The form that is used to convey the buyer's request to purchase is generally a state-approved "Purchase and Sale Agreement" that is accompanied by several exhibits, including a "Seller's Property Disclosure" regarding the condition of the systems of the home, structural and/or repair issues and any other information required to be disclosed by local laws.

The only instance that a disclosure is not part of the agreement is when the property is a bank-owned foreclosure, a pre-foreclosure, or a short sale. Due Diligence is thus placed on the buyer to thoroughly examine the property and make an informed decision whether to proceed with the purchase.

Taking all visible and tangible information into consideration, the primary objective of the buyer and their real estate agent is to establish a pricing strategy. The agent will provide not only comparable sales statistics, current market fluctuations, and information about the seller's motivation, but an experienced understanding of the bidding process.

Right now, buyers and sellers alike are mentally saturated by the media accounts of bargains and steals in the marketplace. While this is true, properties listed for sale have already been significantly discounted because of the pure volume of other distressed sales. The home was selected by the buyer as the home that offered them most of their desired features and benefits at a competitive price. The best advice for the buyer is to establish a final price with the help of their agent and begin negotiations with that end in mind.

Buyers should understand that the seller is not going to give away his home without a realistic price and agreeable terms. By recognizing that this is a mutually acceptable transaction between buyer and seller and not insulting the seller, an equitable result will be reached by all parties. On lender-owned or lender-approved properties, there is generally less negotiating room and more competition. The contract is awarded to the highest bidder with the best terms of purchase.

Once the price and terms of sale are agreed upon and signed by all parties, the buyer will hire a professional home inspector to evaluate the property. The full report will identify every item that does not meet the specifications of today's building code, is not in good working order, or constitutes a health or safety concern and is not otherwise grandfathered.

This is an opportunity for the buyer and real estate professional to review what encompasses a realistic request of repairs for a home that is not new, identify what is a major deficiency, and submit a request to the seller to make necessary repairs. The inspection period is not designed to rebuild the house. When the buyer is realistic with requests, the seller will be more likely to compromise.

Negotiations must end in a win/win situation for all parties. Additionally, if the property is being sold "as is," this is the time to decide whether to move forward with the sale or to terminate the Purchase and Sale Agreement.

The final phases of the home negotiations have thus been completed and it's time to finalize the loan process. The lender will request final documentation on the buyer's financial status and hopefully they did not do something—like purchase a new car or boat or any other big ticket item—that would considerably impact their credit. Though the closing date has been scheduled, there are still a few last-minute details to address.

The buyer must arrange to purchase a home owner's insurance policy. The policy can be paid in advance or is frequently added to the HUD Statement to be paid at closing. The decision to purchase or not purchase title insurance should also be addressed at this time. With the volatility of the market and properties changing ownership through nontraditional sales, it is probably more important than ever to fully understand the importance of purchasing title insurance.

This will be a line item on the HUD as well. It is important to note that title insurance policies should be held for 20 years following the sale of the property and the home owner is still liable for title discrepancies over those twenty years, regardless of whether or not they still own the home.

A successful home purchase and achievement of the American dream is an exciting and rewarding opportunity for the well-prepared buyer who has the right people guiding and educating him along the way. Understanding what to expect eliminates mistakes and maximizes the investment.

About The Author

Lynn Horner Baker

Horner Baker Partners
111 Village Pkwy, Bldg 2, Ste 201
Marietta, GA 30067

(770) 579-4060

sold@lynnhornerbaker.com

www.hornerbakerpartners.com

Lynn Horner Baker has been in the Real Estate business in the Atlanta, GA market since 1991 and has been recognized with multiple awards beginning with "Rookie of the Year" and continuing to being named the number 4 Individual RE/MAX Agent in the state of Georgia and Top 10 Board of Real Estate Agents for the past 18 years.

Having sold thousands of properties in her career, Lynn's primary objective is always to provide excellent service, unparalleled knowledge, and a personal commitment to achieving the financial goals of all buyer and sellers. Currently the owner and President of two Real Estate Brokerages, Lynn is fortunate to work with her son, Chase Horner, who is the Qualifying Broker of both companies. Together they oversee a team of top agents who support Lynn's commitment to excellence.

Lynn speaks and coaches for the Craig Proctor Real Estate Coaching program, a national program that educates real estate professionals throughout North America.

Voted "Woman of the Year" 2010 by the National Association of Professional Women, Lynn is involved in the local chapter of NAPW as well as the East Cobb Business Association and the Golden Retriever Rescue Association. An avid athlete, Lynn will often be seen on the tennis courts or jogging along the Chattahoochee River.

4

Technology for Home Hunters

Kimberlee Canducci

Griffin Realty Group
Plymouth, Massachusetts

Social media and the new technology that supports it have brought profound and positive changes to the real estate industry, removing many of the old constraints on home hunting. It is now easier than ever to find and evaluate real estate using smart phones and iPads. As traditional media like newspapers and magazines have become less effective, Internet-based marketing has driven the development of innovative applications for mobile devices. Video tours of homes are available on YouTube, real estate trends, tips and strategies are on innumerable blogs, and the advent of Google Earth and Google Maps with StreetView allow us to explore every street in a city without leaving our living room. Now, homebuyers can instantly obtain detailed information about homes for sale in the palm of their hand while they're on the road.

According to recent industry figures, it takes an average of 12 weeks and visits to 16 houses before home shoppers find the house they want. But now, as the pace of home buying is approaching the pace of life, the way people search for and buy a home is rapidly evolving. With an ever-growing list of new tools that save time and increase efficiency, buyers and agents can quickly trade information with the click of a button.

There's An App for That!

There are now more people who own a cell phone than those who own a computer. Mobile devices are more than a cool novelty; they are making a fundamental shift in how we communicate. Smart phone applications (commonly referred to as "apps") enable brokers to update home listings, prices, and even share neighborhood information about schools, parks, medical facilities, and recreation.

One of the more revolutionary features in property apps is their ability to detect location by using either GPS technology or a system that determines position relative to Wi-Fi hotspots. Buyers can access information about their immediate surroundings in real time - while they are there - without having to find a computer, set up a laptop, or even type out an address or zip code.

Homebuyers are studying a lot more than just the MLS data. The process of buying a home goes well beyond the basics of searching for the perfect one, getting a mortgage, and handling the logistics of moving. It also involves some of the most basic decisions in people's lives. After all, it's not just real estate that the buyer is acquiring- it's a place to live. The choice they make won't just determine where they live, but also where they'll shop, where their kids will go to school, how long their commute to work will be, and a myriad of other factors that will add to or detract from their quality of life.

Today there are many popular apps, available as free downloads, that can help sort out some of these intangible aspects. Here are a few to check out:

Walk Score - this site helps find "walkable" places to live by displaying a map of what's nearby (schools, groceries, entertainment, etc.) and provides a score for any address to help determine how "car-dependent" a resident would be if they bought a home in that area. Go to www.walkscore.com.

Green Space Map - It used to take a lot of time and research to find information about how close a property may be located to a known EPA site but now that information is available in just moments, plotted on an interactive map. The Green Space Map app provides homebuyers with immediate answers about incidents or problems as reported by the Environmental Protection Agency by showing a property's proximity to reported sites within a 20-mile radius.

Crime Reports - Another factor that heavily influences a buying decision is neighborhood safety. An app called Crime Reports arms homebuyers with crime statistics and provides a national crime map that pinpoints a location using GPS technology. Buyers can see crime data and sex offender addresses plotted on the map for any property they might consider buying.

Criminal Spot - a virtual version of traditional neighborhood watch programs, it's an interactive platform where users update the information. If someone sees suspicious activity in an area, they can report it on Criminal Spot.

Social Media That Matters

If Social media is all about connecting people, then how it's used for home hunting is like a virtual version of old-fashioned "word-of-mouth". By leveraging the millions of connections between people, sites like Facebook and Twitter provide lightening fast dissemination of new listings, trends, and information.

Facebook – Currently there are more than 500 million active users on Facebook and the average user has 130 friends. If Facebook were a country, it would be the third largest in the world with more people than the United States, Canada, and Great Britain combined. YouTube is the world's second largest search engine, and Twitter has 200 million users.

These sites and other social media sites include search engines so users can search other members for information that could be helpful to them. Type "homes for sale" or "real estate agent" into the search field in Facebook, and dozens of hits will come up, each with a list of people who have 'liked' it. These lists can be pure gold for homebuyers; they include lists of people to connect with who may have a home for sale, recommendations for a good real estate broker, and useful information that could impact their decision to buy in a specific region or neighborhood.

Facebook even has its own marketplace to buy and sell almost anything imaginable, including real estate. The Marketplace application page displays the most recent listings and provides easy ways to filter the search, to tailor results to individual needs. It's easy to browse real estate by several different categories, and search for listings from all Marketplace users or by people in a particular social network. It's not hard to see the power of social media, or the burst of speed it can bring to the real estate market.

Foursquare - The line between online games and serious applications is blurring and Foursquare is at the forefront of social media tools that are integrated with GPS technology. It's a fun location-based app that has over 6 million users worldwide and enables homebuyers to find a map of open houses and listings, and see even what else is nearby a property they're currently visiting. They can also "check in" at various homes they visit, earn "badges" and post comments for other visitors and feedback for sellers. Foursquare currently has apps for iPhone, Android, Blackberry and Palm phones, and more are being developed. Go to http://foursquare.com.

QR Codes

These 2D bar codes are popping up everywhere from retail stores, to airline boarding passes, to real estate. The "QR" stands for Quick Response and they create a bridge between the virtual world and reality. In real estate, they're found on lawn signs, in print media, websites, billboards, and business cards. To read them, download a QR reader on your mobile phone. Scanning the code gives the home buyer information about a particular property, a brochure with color photos, and full details about a listing, an open house schedule, a real estate agent, or a website with additional information. Not all QR reader apps are compatible with all phones. A quick Internet search will pull up a list of the different QR readers available and the mobile devices they work on.

Texting is Still King

The typical mobile phone user initiates more text messages than phone calls and 73% of new mobile phone buyers say that text messaging is the most important feature on their phone. It's easy to see why SMS short codes have popped up on real estate signs everywhere.

No longer tied to a laptop computer, mobile users now turn to their smart phone or tablet for information, fueling explosive growth in the need for mobile marketing. For homebuyers, this is another innovation that gives instant access to photos, pricing, and flyers containing additional information. Some providers even have a click-through to a Mobile Optimized Virtual Tour. Successful marketing is all about convenience and making it easy for homebuyers and sellers to get information on their own terms, delivered the way they want it.

Tools, apps, and Internet sites are changing all the time and new ones are created every day. Some things about buying a home will never change, but as technology advances, the way we go about buying them will continue to evolve.

About The Author

Kimberlee Canducci

Griffin Realty Group
385 Court Street
Plymouth, MA 02360

(508) 746-0800

kimcandu@gmail.com
kimcandu@dannygriffin.com

www.KimCandu.com

Kimberlee Canducci is a real estate broker, marketing consultant, speaker, and Internet marketing strategist who leverages the power of on-line marketing to provide her clients with instant, up-to-date information to help them buy or sell .

During her career, Kimberlee co-owned a buyer agency in Southeastern Massachusetts and was featured in Billion Dollar Agent – Lessons Learned, a collection of interviews with 70 top real estate agents who have sold over $1 billion in their career, or are on track to do so. She co-hosted the Smart Home Buying radio show and was a featured guest on Law Talk, a live call-in show about real estate. Kimberlee also produced the Smart Home Buyer Seminars series for four years.

Prior to becoming a real estate agent, she spent 18 years in marketing and sales in the microelectronics industry where she worked on projects that developed her skills in marketing communications. Kimberlee has taken her years of corporate experience in client relations and uses it to bring a professional, results-driven approach to real estate sales.

5

Planning
Your Purchase

Bob Zachmeier
Win3 Realty
Tucson, Arizona

ANSWERS FROM EXPERTS ON BUYING A HOME

Many people buy a home in close proximity to their job, their church, or their children's school. Logically speaking, a home is nothing more than a secure place to keep your belongings and your family, but for most buyers, a lot of emotion is involved in the decision of where to live.

Even though their home is such a large investment, many people spend more time planning their summer vacation than planning their home purchase. A few hours of planning before you start could help avoid overpaying or buying a home that will not be a long-term solution to your needs.

Two Key Questions

Before beginning your search, it is important to have a good understanding of what you are looking for. Most real estate agents search by asking buyers how many bedrooms, bathrooms, and garage stalls they require. Although this structural information is helpful, I've found that the *emotional* reasons for buying a home reveal a lot more about a buyer's needs. Ask yourself these two questions and write at least five answers for each:

What made you choose where you live now?
If you moved, what would you miss the most?

Most buyers' answers are based on emotion rather than structural specifications, especially answers to the second question. For example, knowing that you like to sit on the porch every evening to watch the sunset is an important piece of information that would be totally overlooked if you only considered the size and bedroom count of potential homes.

CHAPTER 5 – PLANNING YOUR PURCHASE

Take the time to consider these questions and capture your thoughts in writing. If you are married, ask your spouse to also create a list and then merge them. The more information you document in this exercise, the better equipped your agent will be to find the perfect home for you.

Planning Ahead

Before buying a home, you should take into account the fact that you'll need to sell it at some time in the future. The issues that concern you now will also be a concern to other buyers when you decide to sell. Busy streets don't usually get any slower or quieter, so consider this fact before making a purchase. Try to envision who will buy your home when you sell several years from now. Understanding your future buyer's needs could help you choose which home to buy now.

Seniors

Many out-of-state people buy a second home in southern locations to escape the harsh northern winters. Most are retired and have no desire to climb stairs in their golden years, so they typically don't purchase multi-level homes. Seniors are concerned about their health, their finances, and their mobility, so they often choose low-maintenance, single-story homes with small yards located near hospitals and city bus lines.

Choosing a multi-level home on a large lot requiring significant yard work could dissuade many seniors from buying your home. With more than 80 million aging baby boomers in the United States, alienating this group could reduce the number of potential buyers by one-third or more!

ANSWERS FROM EXPERTS ON BUYING A HOME

Families

Most families are concerned about the safety of their children so when buying or renting, they avoid homes on busy streets. Families would be most likely to purchase homes with large, grassy, enclosed yards situated in a school district with higher-than-average test scores. Families often opt for multi-story homes because the cost per square foot is lower.

Single level vs. Multi-level

The two most expensive components of a home are the foundation and the roof. A two-story home has half the foundation and half as much roof area as a single story home and thus is much cheaper to build. As mentioned earlier, families are attracted by the affordability and seniors are repelled by the stairs in multi-story homes.

Fixed Costs

The cost of the land your home resides on is a *fixed* cost that isn't changed by the size of the home built on the land. Other fixed costs include the utility lines for gas, electric, water, sewer, phone, and cable television. No matter how big or small the home, these costs remain the same. If you built a 1,000 square foot home the fixed costs would be divided over 1,000 feet of living area, but on a 2,000 square foot home, the same fixed costs would be spread over twice the area and thus the cost per square foot would be lower.

Building Materials and Amenities

Variable costs change depending on the amount and quality of the building materials used in the home. Variable costs include concrete, lumber, sheetrock, and paint.

Buyers will often pay extra for improvements like swimming pools and extra garage stalls, but energy efficient windows and extra insulation typically do not have much affect on the price buyers will pay. Few upgrades increase the sale price by as much as they cost to install, so finding a home that already has the upgrades you want is usually less expensive than adding the amenities after the purchase.

Establishing Value

In a free market economy, *market value* is defined as the amount a buyer is willing to pay and a seller is willing to accept. Because it takes both a buyer and a seller to strike a deal, a home's value is determined by the supply and demand of the market, not the buyer, the seller, or their agents.

If hundreds of homes are available for sale but only a small percentage of them are being sold each month, the imbalance is deemed to be a "buyer's market". To sell in an oversupplied market where there are far fewer buyers than there are homes for sale, sellers must either add value by providing favorable financing or lower their asking price below the price of competing homes.

Conversely, a "seller's market" exists when a large percentage of the available homes are sold each month. In this environment, buyers must often pay more than the seller's asking price in order to beat other buyers' offers to purchase the home. In this situation, homes in excellent condition and priced competitively can create "bidding wars" that drive prices tens of thousands higher than the seller's asking price.

Zeroing In On Your Target

Don't rely on the news media to determine whether you are in a buyer's market or a seller's market. There are several factors that need to be considered before buying a home or even choosing the area in which to live. A little research can help you determine where and what type of property to buy in order to get the best value now and the highest probable appreciation in the future.

You'll need to know how many homes are listed for sale in the area and how many are selling each month. With this information you can calculate the *percentage* of available inventory being sold each month. Try to get this data from your real estate agent for the past two to five years to establish whether you can time your purchase around seasonal trends when there are fewer buyers in the market.

You'll also need to find out what portion of the overall sales are town homes, condos, mobile homes, and single family homes. Depending on which type of property you intend to buy, you'll want to calculate the percentage of available properties of that type being sold each month. After finding all of the sales of the property type you intend to purchase, divide them into $25,000 price increments.

Are the properties in your price range in areas where you want to live? Where is the highest percentage of available inventory being sold? Have sale prices been increasing or decreasing over the past two years? Are the properties that are selling in need of repair? If so, how much was the price discounted on the properties requiring repairs?

These questions will help you understand where the highest demand exists, whether prices are increasing or decreasing, and whether it is worth buying a home in need of repairs. Most buyers who are willing to purchase homes needing repairs expect the price to be much lower than the homes that don't need to be repaired. Since the demand is highest for properties that are well maintained and don't need repairs, expect to pay a higher price for these properties.

Finding a Bargain

Many homeowners believe that they need to offer less than the seller is asking in order to get a good deal. This belief overlooks the fact that the most desperate homeowners who need to sell quickly actually price their homes *below* market value. Underpriced homes often sell higher than the asking price because educated buyers know that even if they pay more than the seller is asking, it is still the best value.

Rather than offering less than the asking price, wise buyers offer *more* for well-priced homes to ensure that they get them. Buyers who offer less than the already discounted price are often outbid, especially on newly-listed properties that haven't been exposed to weekend showing activity.

Missing the Mark

I once listed a bank-owned property where the seller really missed the mark and priced the property $50,000 lower than we suggested. On the Tuesday the property was listed, we received an offer that was $2,000 lower than the asking price. The bank had a policy of not accepting offers lower than the asking price during the first ten days on the market, so they declined the buyer's offer. Over the weekend, this underpriced home attracted *sixteen* other offers and ended up selling to another buyer for $50,000 more than the asking price.

If the first buyer would have submitted a full price offer, they would have secured this amazing bargain before anyone else found it. By trying to save $2,000 they gave other buyers the opportunity to outbid them. Their bargain hunting cost them the $50,000 in equity they would have realized on the first day of owning the home.

Unfortunately, many buyers don't learn this lesson until after they've lost the home they really want to buy. They end up paying more money for a home that is less desirable than their first choice. Don't let this happen to you! Find an agent who is willing to educate you about the market by providing data that helps you make intelligent offers from the start.

Divide the available inventory of homes into four categories; excellent, good, fair, and poor. Whether you rank the homes by how good of a value they are or by their condition, each category will represent 25% of the available properties on the market. Given a choice, if the location, size, amenities, and price are comparable, most buyers will choose the nicest home with the least problems at the best price.

If 35% of available properties are selling each month, all that remain are the bottom 15% of the "good" properties, the "fair" properties, and the "poor" properties. Homes that are the best value <u>always</u> sell first, so when you find the perfect home, don't wait to make an offer!

About The Author

Bob Zachmeier

Win3 Realty
2474 E River Road
Tucson, AZ 85718

(520) 690-WIN3

bob@win3realty.com

www.win3realty.com

Bob Zachmeier was born and raised in Mandan, ND. His parents showed by example that determination and a strong work ethic could achieve almost any goal.

As the third of six children, Zachmeier learned early in life to become self-reliant. At the age of sixteen, he owned a fireworks business, complete with billboard and radio advertising. The business helped fund his college education and that of several siblings.

He became a part-time real estate agent in 2000 at the age of forty. In 2002, he was earning enough from real estate investments to leave his job as a manufacturing engineer after twenty-two-years at Texas Instruments and later Raytheon's Defense Electronics division in Tucson, Arizona.

In 2004, Zachmeier and his wife, Camille, founded Win3 Realty. The name reflects their desire to create a win-win-win situation for their clients, the community, and the agents, staff, and owners of their company.

Four years after starting Win3 Realty, their team was number one among 6,000 agents in overall sales and buyer-side transactions. With only twelve agents on their team, they've continually pushed the bar higher; selling more than 2,000 homes in the tough Arizona market between 2008 and 2011.

Zachmeier shares his success with others by speaking at national conferences and by holding real estate training seminars for agents across North America. His events have produced over $100,000 for children's charities like the Make-A-Wish Foundation and Boys and Girls Clubs of America. Zachmeier co-founded REO4Kids, an elite national group of real estate agents who give proceeds from every sale to children's charities. In 2010, he and Camille received the "Spirit of Philanthropy" award from the Association of Fundraising Professionals.

By sharing his experience and practical advice as a real estate broker, coach, college instructor, author, lecturer, and philanthropist, Bob Zachmeier has helped thousands of people improve their financial well-being.

Zachmeier has written and published two other books; Upside Up Real Estate Investing™ and Sold On Change™ To find additional titles, visit the publisher's website at www.outoftheboxbooks.com. You can also contact the author via e-mail: <bob@bobzachmeier.com>.

6

Home Inspection Tips

Dawn McCurdy

McCurdy Real Estate Group
Latham, New York

What is a Home Inspection?

A home inspection, also referred to as a "structural inspection," is by definition an examination and assessment of the condition of a home. Although not required by law, it is strongly recommended to conduct a home inspection. A home inspector examines the home's condition, evaluating its structure, plumbing, electric, heating and air-conditioning systems. Home inspectors inform buyers about what kind of repairs are needed before they buy a home, as well as how to avoid future problems.

Does a Buyer Need a Home Inspection?

If a buyer tries to save money by refusing to pay for a home inspection, they may be losing money in the long run. A home inspection can uncover potential problems that can, if left untreated, lead to costly repairs. A buyer should never let the apparent beauty of a home mislead them into thinking that the home may not have significant defects.

For example, some sellers may advertise that they have a "new roof" when in fact, only the <u>shingles</u> may be new. They may have neglected to inform you that the damaged plywood and old shingles were left underneath the new shingles, which could significantly reduce the life expectancy of the roof. This is why mortgage lenders sometimes require an inspection before approving a loan.

When to Get an Inspection

Without question, an inspection should be done before the buyer closes on the purchase and takes possession of the home. There should be a clause in the real-estate contract that makes the sale of the home contingent upon the inspection. A buyer should be sure to have an inspection performed in the time-frame specified in the contract. If the inspection deadline is not met, buyers waive their right to recover their earnest money if an inspection uncovers major deal-breaking issues.

A reasonable time frame would be within a two-week period from acceptance of the buyer's offer and, typically, is at the buyer's expense. However, a buyer shouldn't wait until they have placed an offer on a house before beginning the search for a home inspector.

If a buyer waits until that point, and cannot find an acceptable inspector to schedule in the required time frame, the buyer will only have two choices: go with an inspector that is not their first choice, or risk running past the deadline for the inspection (which could void any chance of having the seller take care of repairs). Neither is an acceptable option!

Are Home Inspections Worth the Cost?
The value and necessity of an extensive home inspection cannot be emphasized enough. Many home buyers have attempted to save the $200 – $500 cost of a good inspection, but have spent enormous amounts of money repairing items that any reputable home inspector would have pointed out.

Inspections often disclose defects in the property that could materially affect its safety, livability, or resale value. A buyer should not let anyone—not an agent, nor their family or friends, and especially not the home seller—discourage them from having the property thoroughly inspected.

As long as the contract is written with a contingency for an acceptable inspection, any defects in the home must be either repaired, or the buyer may elect to receive monetary compensation to make the repairs. If the buyer is not satisfied, they have the option to cancel the purchase contract.

How to Find the Right Inspector?

Not all home inspectors are equally qualified, and choosing the right inspector is crucial. A buyer has a myriad of resources available in making this decision. A good place to start is with a real estate agent. If a buyer chooses their agent wisely, the agent can recommend good, reliable inspectors. A good tip is to obtain three or four names and addresses of inspectors that the agent's other customers have used, rather than accepting just one recommendation.

A buyer can also ask friends, family, and co-workers for referrals. A buyer might also call their mortgage lender or their lawyer for recommendations. Sometimes, a buyer has a friend or family member that is qualified to conduct this service and trusts them to do it. It is wise, though, not to have this person as the sole inspector. Instead, they should accompany a professional inspector as an additional resource.

Another option for a buyer is to use a home inspector who is certified by a national home inspection organization. These groups establish professional standards for their members to follow. Inspectors who belong to the organizations listed below have met rigorous testing and experience requirements, and are among the nation's most qualified professionals in this field.

Professional Home Inspection organizations include:

- American Society of Home Inspectors (ASHI), www.ashi.org
- National Association of Certified Home Inspectors (NACHI), www.nachi.org
- National Association of Home Inspectors, Inc. (NAHI), www.nahi.org

What to Look for in a Home Inspector

Once a buyer has compiled their top two or three choices, they can move onto phone interviews to make their final decision. It is very important to find an inspector who is understandable and who communicates well.

Request a sample inspection report first, to ensure that it is easy to read and provides the information you expect. Buyers should look for a few key things in reviewing sample inspection reports: Does it give the ages of specific systems in the house or just an idea of their current state? Does it estimate the cost of repairs and remedies for existing problems? Many inspectors don't provide written repair quotes but it is important to know the price range of potential repairs.

It is advisable to inquire about the exact methods that the inspector uses: Do they actually go on the roof or into the crawl space under the house? Some check these areas as a matter of course, but others charge extra, and still others will not go closer to the roof than standing in the driveway, looking up, and jotting down notes from there. A buyer needs to know exactly what they are getting when they pay for an inspection.

Does the inspection company carry any type of liability insurance to cover any damage to the house created by the inspector during his tour, or major defects the home inspector misses? If not, the buyer may want to consider finding a company that does.

How Much Does a Home Inspection Cost?

A buyer shouldn't hire the cheapest inspector they can find, as better inspectors will typically charge more, and the better inspectors are usually worth the additional cost. If a lower-priced inspector misses even one problem that a more expensive—but experienced—inspector would find, then you've lost money.

Home inspections can range from $200 to $500. The price will vary from one region to another, on the square footage and age of the property, on possible optional services (such as septic, well, and radon testing), and the individual inspector's or inspection company's rates. This is a small expense compared to the large investment of purchasing a home.

It is helpful to have gathered, prior to the time of the inspection, any property condition disclosures provided by the seller, a list of any repairs or improvements done on the home, and potential warranty information. The inspector can use this information as a reference point to determine if certain tests should be performed at an additional expense, based upon the home maintenance records.

Additional testing for radon, asbestos, well-water contamination, or mold usually costs more than a basic inspection. The home inspector might direct a buyer to someone else for those reports, perhaps to an individual or company that specializes in the inspection of environmental hazards.

Payment is required at the time of service, no matter what the findings. A buyer should view this as a cheap insurance policy. Although, there may be nothing wrong now, it is for the buyer's protection to make this modest investment.

Who Should Attend the Inspection?
The buyer should attend the inspection, as attending the home inspection will allow them to come away with a better understanding of any potential problems, while learning a lot about the house in the process. The buyer should be cautious of inspectors and agents who discourage them from attending the inspection. Any good inspector will want the client to attend. If the buyer is working with a real estate agent, then the agent should also be present.

It is ideal if a buyer can request that the home owner <u>not</u> be present during most of the inspection. It will allow the buyer freedom to probe and inspect all the details of the home without feeling that they are being invasive of the home-owner's privacy. If the home owner arrives at the end, it can be helpful, as sometimes they can provide information about the home's history to which an inspector would not be privy.

The inspection is typically the last time that the buyer is allowed in the home prior to closing, so a buyer should take all the time that they need to feel comfortable with this major decision. It may be advisable to bring a camera, video camera, measuring tape, and memo board. Although the inspector will provide a very thorough report, a buyer may have some "non-structural notes" that will be helpful to review later.

A buyer should be observant of items that remain with the home such as window treatments, built-ins, appliances and overall aesthetic condition. A buyer may also observe colors, document door and window locations, and measure rooms to plan for furniture placement.

What to Do During an Inspection

In short, take notes on what the inspector says could be foreseeable problems with the house. The inspector's job is to find defects that a typical layman may not be able to detect. This is not meant to be a pass/fail type of test. Simply put, an inspector is there, as the buyer's representative, to make observations and recommendations based upon the conditions found.

The inspector's job is to bring to light any important problems with the house. With this information, a buyer might still choose to purchase the house, but will have room to negotiate the price. They can say to the owner, "The inspector says the roof is in poor condition, and he estimates it is well over eighteen years old, so it's overdue for replacement." In negotiations, such comments can help lower the price.

The time frame will vary depending on the number and type of inspections, as well as the size of the home. An inspection typically takes two to four hours, and covers the following areas: mechanical and safety items, structural features (like the foundation), plumbing systems, heating, cooling, and ventilation systems, major appliances, roof, electrical, attic and the exterior of the home, including driveways and fences.

What to Expect After the Inspection

The inspector will compile the findings in a typed report and provide it to whoever commissioned the job (usually the buyer). Most companies will deliver this report to the buyer immediately on site or within a few days. The buyer should provide a copy of the report immediately to their attorney and real estate agent.

It is best to keep this report confidential until these representatives have had a chance to decipher the information and advise the buyer on their next move. The seller or seller's agent may request a copy of this report, but it should not be supplied—not at this time. The buyer's attorney (or agent if attorneys are not used) will provide a copy, along with proper notifications to accompany the report of any items found.

How to Negotiate Repairs?

The buyer's agent or attorney will negotiate any repairs, cash credits, or advise the buyer to walk away if the home inspection reflects too many problems. This determination will be dependent upon independent contractor's or exterminator's estimates to repair the damages highlighted in the report.

The sellers may provide these estimates, and it is advisable to keep them. The buyer's attorney or real estate agent will typically offer referrals of reputable contractors to choose from. There may be a time period allowed in the contract to obtain these estimates, usually ranging from 10 to 14 days.

Access to the home will be allowed to the buyer to conduct the evaluation. The buyer and their agent should accompany the contractor to fully understand the scope of the work potentially needed and answer any questions. Items to have present at this time are the contract for sale, the structural inspection report, and any estimates the seller may have provided as a reference to ensure all questionable items are addressed.

All estimates should be in writing and supplied to the buyer's attorney and agent. Unless the property is being purchased in "as-is" condition, it is common to re-negotiate the contract based upon the repair estimates. It will ultimately be up to the buyer to decide if they want to move forward, and what terms are acceptable should there be a major defect. Laws in each state will vary as to what constitutes a "major defect," based on a set dollar amount in the purchase and sale contract.

If repairs are done prior to closing, the buyer should get another inspection after the problem has been fixed, and obtain any receipts, work orders and warranties that may apply. If the buyer opts for a credit, the contract may need to be re-written to reflect these changes. A buyer should discuss the best way to include these concessions with their lender, real estate agent and attorney, who will advise the best solution that meets the buyer's financial needs. All agreements need to be in writing, either by an attorney letter or an executed addendum by all parties.

The goal of this process is to create a win-win atmosphere. The purchase of a home is an emotional process for both the buyer and seller. It is human nature that no one wants to "lose" a negotiation.

A win-win negotiation allows both parties to feel that they have given something, while the other party also has made concessions. Buyers and sellers alike want to feel that they are getting a fair deal. A buyer, keeping this in mind during the inspection negotiation, increases the probability of a successful outcome for all parties.

About The Author

Dawn McCurdy

McCurdy Real Estate Group
1004 New Loudon Rd, PO Box 456
Latham, NY 12110

(518) 785-9900 - Office
(518) 441-3538 - Mobile

dmccurdy@mccurdyrealestate.com

www.mccurdyrealestate.com

Dawn McCurdy was born and raised in Albany, NY and has been selling real estate in the Capital Region since 1985. She is Broker/Owner of The McCurdy Real Estate Group, Inc. and has helped more than 3,000 families. Her business is founded on trust from past clients, who refer their friends and family.

McCurdy leads a team of like-minded colleagues who she coaches to continually bring their businesses to the next level. She is a mentor to her agents as well as many in the industry. Dawn's commitment to her clients and her team is to overcome everyday challenges using her strengths, skills, talents, energy and enthusiasm to their advantage.

Dawn holds many real estate designations, a Paralegal degree and belongs to numerous local organizations. Being a director of her local Chamber, she is very involved in her community and contributes to multiple charities on a local and national level. Dawn resides in Colonie, NY with her husband, Phil, and two beautiful twin daughters, Amber & Taylor.

7

What Your Agent Needs to <u>Know</u>!

Amy Coleman
Golden State Realty Group
Sacramento, California

ANSWERS FROM EXPERTS ON BUYING A HOME

When shopping for their first or next home, most people have two goals. They want to find the perfect home to meet their needs and purchase it at the lowest possible price. Isn't that what everyone wants?

You can find great deals in any real estate market. You just need to know what to look for and where to look! Working with a knowledgeable real estate agent can save time and money enabling dreams that otherwise might not be accessible.

Before looking at homes, find an agent who regularly tracks the local market and can explain whether the market in a specific area is declining or on the rise. Agents with their thumb on the pulse of the market are able to spot minor changes long before others see them coming. They can provide a view of the overall market or a detailed view of a specific neighborhood or zip code.

Buying a home is the largest financial commitment most people make in their lives. Wouldn't the decision to purchase in one area over another be easier if an expert provided the data and trend analysis to prove that you were making the right decision? If you understood the seasonal tendencies of the housing market and how the economy and interest rates were affecting home values at different price points, your decisions of when to buy, what to buy, and how much to offer would be much easier.

To start the hunt for the perfect home, find a real estate agent who has the most information about the market area in which you plan to live. If you planned to purchase a home in

California, would you rely on market information from your real estate agent cousin in New York? Your cousin might be able to provide negotiating techniques that are common in their market, but they will not be able to provide much insight on the common practices, forms, necessary disclosures, and trends that are specific to the California market.

Although real estate licenses are issued by each state, would you really want to rely on information from a real estate agent in Los Angeles if you intended to purchase a home in Sacramento? Los Angeles and Sacramento are worlds away even though they are in the same state. Housing trends, local disclosures, what is hot, and what is not will vary from area to area. Find the area where you want to live and choose the most knowledgeable agent in that area.

For assistance with the most expensive decision you will make in your lifetime, it makes sense to hire a full-time experienced agent who has made a career out of helping people buy and sell their homes. Most people would agree that a full-time real estate agent whose livelihood depends upon referrals from satisfied clients would be better equipped to help you than someone who sells a home or two per year on weekends.

Look for an agent who will take the time to determine your specific requirements. Most agents only ask their clients about price range, square footage, and the number of bedrooms or bathrooms desired. These structural details may assist the agent in searching for a property, but they don't address the reason people fall in love with their homes.

ANSWERS FROM EXPERTS ON BUYING A HOME

When you purchase a home, you are creating a lifestyle. An experienced agent will ask what made you choose the home or apartment where you currently live and whether those things are still important to you. Another crucial question to be asked is what you will miss most about your present home after you leave. The answers to these questions will provide the agent with a good understanding of exactly what you are looking for.

This analysis reveals many aspects you may not have thought about. It can reveal desirable school districts, proximity to bus lines and retail establishments that might not have been discussed previously. This information enables your agent to customize their search to locate the perfect home for you and your family.

Buying a home can be an emotional roller coaster! It is important to have the entire process explained from start to finish before you begin your search. If you know what to expect, the wait doesn't seem as long, and you'll encounter much less stress. If an agent is not willing to spend time upfront to listen and understand your needs, find someone else who will!

A good agent will also provide a market analysis and set an expectation of how much you will need to pay to get the amenities that are important to you. By doing all of this upfront, planning before becoming emotionally attached to a home will enable you to make more logical decisions and avoid overpaying when you find the perfect home.

Agents who show their clients homes that are beyond their price range do them a huge disservice. After previewing homes that are substantially more than you can afford, it will be difficult to find a home with similar amenities in your price range. Spending time to review market graphs and charts before your search begins will help you understand whether the area is a Seller's Market, where properties sell quickly, or a Buyer's Market, where few homes are selling. This will help you decide whether it is the right time to buy.

The key to starting a successful home-buying process is determining the area you want to live in and the type of home you can afford to buy. As simple as this may sound, many home buyers don't take the time to do this before they start shopping.

There are questions you should consider as you get started. How much of your paycheck would you be willing to commit to a house payment? How much are you paying now? How many bedrooms do you need and how would you like them positioned? Do you want to live on one side of the freeway vs. the other? What part of the city are you most interested in? These are the kinds of questions you should ask, as well as having a good understanding of the type of market you are in.

In a Seller's market with a significant shortage of available homes, you may need to offer more than the asking price and may end up in an auction-like bidding war for a desirable home. Knowing how much you would be willing to pay before you enter into a situation like this is highly advisable. Knowing the price that similar homes in the area have sold for and how long it took them to sell will provide you with a good understanding of each specific neighborhood.

In a Buyer's market it is important to know if the home has been on the market for a long time and whether there have been recent price reductions. Many times, sellers will overprice their home and it sits unsold for several months. This causes potential buyers to question whether something is wrong with the property. As a local expert, your agent will be able to help you determine when the last price reduction occurred, possibly why it occurred, and how close your offer should be to the asking price in order to be considered.

If your agent does not know their local market then you may fall into the trap of "Bidding Blind." What price should you offer when you bid on a home? Is the seller's asking price too high, or is it a great deal at the current price? If you don't have current information about how many similar homes are available and the price at which they are selling, you could easily overpay for your home or lose it to another buyer because your offer was too low. Good deals don't last long in any market, so you'll want to have the data readily available to help you make well-informed decisions.

When you have a good understanding of the market, your agent can help you navigate past the over-priced homes and zero in on the great deals. As you view homes with your agent, you will begin to recognize which homes are good values and which are over-priced. The homes you view can usually be placed in one of four categories:

Clearly Over-priced:

Every seller wants the most money they can get for their home, and real estate agents know this. If several agents are competing for the listing, an easy way to win the job is to offer to list the home for more than it is worth. Unfortunately, this is done far too often and many homes are priced 10-20% over their true value.

This is not in the seller's best interest, because the market is seldom fooled. Over-pricing a home will cause the property to languish on the market for months or years, causing the seller to chase the market downward. This strategy relies on buyers who have not done their research and unknowingly purchase the over-priced home. Buyers BEWARE!

Somewhat Over-priced:

Believe it or not, about 75% of the homes on the market are 5-10% overpriced! These homes stay on the market longer than they should for two reasons; either the seller believes that their home is really worth this much, despite what the market has indicated, OR the seller has left room in their price for negotiation.

Either way, this strategy will cost them unnecessary time, energy, and stress. Countering back and forth between the buyer and seller can be exhausting, and you never know whether the person at the other end of the negotiation is about to give in or give up! You could spend weeks negotiating on a home only to lose it.

Meanwhile, the perfect home may have been listed and sold while you were negotiating with an unrealistic seller. The best advice is to review the numbers, make an offer, and determine from the seller's initial response whether or not they are realistic. If not, move on!

Priced Correctly at Market Value:

Logical sellers understand that real estate is subject to the law of supply and demand. These sellers price their homes at a realistic value based on a thorough analysis of other homes that have sold, are under contract, or currently available for sale. These competitively priced homes usually sell in a reasonable time and very close to the asking price. This is the perfect situation for a buyer, especially first-time buyers, because the emotional stress and bantering are not necessary.

By the time most buyers have viewed a few homes, they have a pretty good understanding of value. To ensure that you don't become emotionally attached to an over-priced home, preview those that seem to be priced competitively before looking at those that seem to be over-priced.

Priced Below Fair Market Value:

Some sellers are very motivated and have compelling reasons to sell quickly. Whatever is driving the need to sell is usually more important than getting a high price for their home. Significantly under-pricing a home can attract multiple offers in a matter of hours and the home will usually sell very quickly.

Often times a "bidding war" ensues between interested buyers. The seller may ask for the "highest and best" offer from each of the interested parties. Since you have no idea how much the other buyers will offer, it is hard to decide how much to offer.

In situations like this, it is very important to have an agent who knows the market, can guide you on how much to offer, and keep you from over-paying like many buyers do at auctions. Although it is emotionally difficult, make your best educated offer and hope for the best.

Paying too much can turn your dream home into a nightmare. Utilizing the services of an experienced buyer's agent can keep you from overpaying for a home, losing the home you want to another buyer or worse yet, buying the wrong home for your needs.

Take the time to find a qualified agent who is honest, ethical, and knows the market where you want to live. This will help take the fear out of the equation so that you can make an educated purchase on a great home. Shopping for a home can be exhilarating when you have a professional agent to guide you through the home-buying process.

About The Author

Amy Coleman

Golden State Realty Group
3835 N Freeway Blvd. Suite 140
Sacramento, CA 95834

(916) 960-1774

amy@colemanhammer.com

www.sacramentohousefinder.com

Amy Coleman was born and raised in Sacramento and attended Sacramento's top notch Business Marketing Program at California State University. While in college, she consulted, marketed and managed cosmetics for a nationwide chain. Amy has a passion for people and a natural ability to listen to their needs, explain their options, and convert them to friends.

In 1999, Amy found an opportunity in real estate that utilized her marketing degree, her outgoing personality, and allowed her to help others achieve their dream of home ownership. Amy continues to educate herself to provide her clients and friends with innovative choices that best fit their needs. Amy also owns a property management firm to assist clients in managing wealth-building investment properties.

Amy ranks in the top 1% of all agents in Sacramento's tri-county area. She gives back to the community by supporting the Make-A-Wish Foundation, Boys and Girls Club of America, and other children's charities. She co-owns Golden State Real Estate with her business partner, Bruce Hammer.

8

Buyer Agency and Buyer Agents

Frank Profeta
Homeside Realty Group
Bohemia, New York

Every prospective home buyer should consider being represented by a buyer agent when purchasing a home, as there are numerous benefits to doing so. In most states, a home buyer would not even think about purchasing a home without a buyer agent; in others, though, it is a foreign concept that many buyers cannot seem to comprehend.

This chapter will detail the benefits of selecting the best buyer agent and will provide an overview of the many elements involved in an exclusive buyer agency agreement.

#1: Loyalty
An exclusive buyer agent will give the home buyer 100% loyalty, as it is their fiduciary responsibility to represent the buyer's best interests—and nobody else's. In a real estate transaction involving a listing agent, the seller has hired that agent to represent their best interests. Why wouldn't a buyer have their own agent to represent *their* best interests?

A buyer agent only looks out for the buyer's best interests, and not the seller or listing agent's interests. If a buyer expresses an interest in a particular home and is not represented by a buyer agent, the listing agent is only obligated to tell the truth, and that is it.

The buyer may be missing out on a wealth of relevant information, as the seller's agent is working for the seller, and will not go out of their way to help them.

#2: Finding the Best Deal

An exclusive buyer agent will find a buyer the best deal within their budget and desired area. The agent will have market knowledge and know where to find the best deals. Most buyers think real estate agents can only show them homes that are on the Multiple Listing Service (MLS), but that just isn't true.

A good buyer agent can show all the homes from all real estate companies whether exclusive or on the MLS, as well as homes that are not on the MLS, such as those that are "for sale by owner." This is a benefit most buyers are unaware of, and will give the buyer a distinct advantage when working with an exclusive buyer agent.

For example: why would a real estate agent that is not an exclusive buyer agent want to show a for-sale-by-owner home? Because they don't have the buyer's loyalty or the seller's, they would run the risk of not getting paid. With a buyer agency agreement in place, the buyer and their agent are committed to one another and neither have a fear of loss.

Even better, the buyer gains good representation. For example, a skilled agent can take a buyer through the for-sale-by-owner's home, ask all the right questions, get all the necessary information to give the buyer the upper hand when negotiating the deal. A good buyer agent is worth their weight in gold.

#3: Negotiating the Deal

The buyer agent will not only negotiate the best possible price—they will also negotiate the best *terms*. Most home buyers think only about price, but there is more to negotiating a good deal than just price.

Some common examples would be closing date, contract date, home inspection, repairs, and the amount of the down payment, which is something that is overlooked far too often. The seller's agent is trying to get the buyer to pay as high of a down payment as possible because it will make the contract more secure for the seller. Should something happen, it is less likely that the buyer would walk away from a larger contract deposit.

What about the buyer's interests? What about contract security for the buyer? A good buyer agent will split the total down payment by negotiating a minimum down payment on formal contract and the remainder on closing.

This is very smart to do, should a disagreement arise, an unforeseen circumstance occur, or anything else that could cause the buyer not to close, possibly allowing the seller to keep the buyer's earnest money. The less money the buyer has tied up in earnest money, the better, so they can move right to the next transaction without skipping a beat.

In seeing the advantages of working with a buyer agent, every home buyer should understand the benefits and advantages of exclusive buyer agency. However, the buyer may still have a few questions.

The most common question that prospective buyers have about working with an agent is, "how do I find the right exclusive buyer agent?" Typically, the best way is by recommendation. When a buyer begins the home-buying process, they often begin by speaking to friends and family. Many will share their own experiences—the good as well as the bad. Through this avenue, the buyer may pick up a few good names, as well as a few to steer clear of.

If a buyer doesn't have a referral for a good buyer agent, the next place to look is online at the local Real Estate Board website. Many boards have their members' information online, where anybody can access the agents' experience and service areas.

Once a buyer has selected a few names, it is time to call them and ask a few simple questions. Every buyer should ask their prospective agent the following key questions, along with anything else that may be of importance:

- How much experience do they have representing buyers?
- How many buyers have they successfully helped in the last 12 months?
- How long have they been selling in the area in which the buyer is looking?
- What sources other than MLS do they use to locate properties of interest?

- Can they give you priority access daily to all the hot new listings as soon as they hit the market?
- Will they give you addresses so you can drive by ahead of time and see the homes from the outside first?
- How much contact will they have with you through the entire process, from house hunting to closing?

Once the buyer feels comfortable with their new buyer agent, it is time to meet them and enter into a buyer agency agreement. Before doing so, you will want to make sure to cover a few key elements in the buyer agency agreement. These elements include:

- A good and accurate written description of the type of home that the buyer is looking for, including the condition of the home and most importantly, the price of the home.

- The term of the agreement—most buyer agency agreements last 6-12 months. This length of time should not seem daunting, as it will give the buyer the time they need to find a good deal without the pressure of time constraints.

- The amount of the buyer agent's commission, which will vary slightly from area to area. An average buyer agent will charge an average fee while a good buyer agent will charge a higher fee—in other words, when it comes to agents, you get what you pay for!

Every buyer should keep in mind that a good agent will find the best deal and negotiate the best terms and conditions. Most buyer agency agreements have a provision that allows the buyer agent to negotiate for the seller to pay the fee on the buyer's behalf.

There is a big difference between an amateur and a professional—the professional knows the ins-and-outs of the real estate business, and can put that knowledge to work for you. The value and benefit of a skilled buyer agent will far exceed the buyer agency fee. Home buyers who employ a skilled agent will look back and be glad that they did.

About The Author

Frank Profeta

Homeside Realty Group
80 Orville Drive, Suite 100
Bohemia, NY 11716

(631) 289-5151

frank@frankprofeta.com

www.frankprofeta.com

Frank Profeta has been selling homes on Long Island, NY since August, 1991. In April, 1996, he started his own real estate company out of his bedroom in his parents' home. Currently, Frank is ranked in the Top 10 among more than 24,000 real estate professionals on Long Island.

Frank's philosophy at Homeside Realty Group differs from most other brokerages. He has a "pay it forward" mentality and believes it is imperative to give back to his local community through educating the cooperating brokers, agents, homebuyers, and investors.

Frank has formed a *team* of agents and support staff, rather than emulating traditional brokerages that focus on getting as many agents working for them as possible. He is very selective and chooses only the most talented people who want to work towards one common goal: finding clients the best home for the best price in the least amount of time.

9

Assembling
A Dream Team

Chase Horner
Horner Baker Partners
Marietta, Georgia

ANSWERS FROM EXPERTS ON BUYING A HOME

First-time buyers, move-up buyers, luxury buyers and seasoned investors alike must repeat the following: "Buying a home is a *process*, not an event."

It is an intricate process with many moving parts, requiring patience, expertise, strict adherence to deadlines, and, above all, organization. Anyone thinking about buying a home must be prepared for what many would consider the most important purchase of a lifetime, taking seriously the responsibilities that such a large purchase entails. The wise buyer will assemble a "dream team" early on, form a strategy, and execute the plan.

With all the misinformation, Monday morning-quarterbacking, and foot-in-mouth prognostications media outlets have broadcast in the last five years, there is one fact that stands rock solid: in the long and storied history of the American housing market (and even back before records were kept), there has never been a better time to buy a home.

Taking the emotion out of the home-buying process, if only for a minute, one can see that buying a home takes a sophisticated team of professionals, including a seasoned real estate broker knowledgeable in the target market, a mortgage lender in command of current economic forces, loan products, and the ability to accurately articulate technical financial terminology in laymen's terms, local attorneys, escrow firms, title companies specializing in "closing" a real estate transaction, as well as appraisers and inspectors, just to name a few. Clearly, it takes a team to complete the home-buying process.

CHAPTER 9 – ASSEMBLING A DREAM TEAM

The initial phase of the buying process should begin by shaking the money tree. Buyers should first meet and interview legitimate lenders to get pre-qualified for a loan. Consider a federally-insured bank or a NCUA-insured credit union and obtain a loan application, good faith estimate (GFE) and a credit score disclosure.

The lender will determine the purchaser's buying ability based upon work history, earnings history, current savings, debt-to-income ratios (current liabilities), down payment capacity, and savings reserves post-closing. Obviously, credit scores will not only impact the loan interest rate, but also will determine if a buyer will qualify for a conventional or FHA loan. The minimum credit score for an FHA loan is lower, but includes more up-front fees to offset the risk.

The minimum credit score for a 97% Homepath loan (Fannie Mae's proprietary product) loan is usually slightly higher. For a standard conventional loan with a loan-to-value of 95% or higher, buyers will typically need an even higher credit score to obtain mortgage insurance. The lender will establish sales price, loan amount, and loan payment amounts based upon guidelines that calculate the buyer's maximum debt limit.

Obtaining a home loan can be a full-time job, making it a part of the process where the buyer must exercise some patience. In today's financial climate, lenders will require a ton of documentation, including income and asset documents, pay stubs, each numbered page of the last two bank statements, IRA and 401K statements, brokerage account statements, income tax returns from the past few years, and other tax forms. Potential buyers should be advised to start saving the actual statements as lenders don't like internet printouts. Basically you'll need everything just short of a DNA sample.

The reason for this is simple — the banks want to ensure a return on their investment and mitigate any potential borrower default. A couple of last tips for serious buyers: don't close any revolving credit cards before beginning to shop for a house; don't apply for new credit cards, car loans or department store charge cards; and don't let any account go into collection. It's also a good idea for buyers to always pay insurance co-payments at the time of doctor's visits.

Without getting too far down the money road, buyers need to consider "the product," and the real estate broker needed to help them find it. Of course, everybody wants to feel like they are getting a good deal on a home, so buyers will need to decide if their goal is a generally better-conditioned resale property, a short sale (which should be nationally rebranded as a long sale because there is nothing short about a process that sometimes takes months), an REO/Foreclosure property sold in "as-is" condition, an auction property sold on the county courthouse steps, or at a ballroom event with hundreds of other bidders, or a HUD home.

In any scenario, you need to understand your opponent (sometimes referred to as a selling partner, because the process demands considerable cooperation from the other side) while remaining realistic with your offers: is a "mom-and-pop" seller going to be ready to negotiate in today's real estate reality?

Buyers should ask themselves other questions, such as whether the bank is ready to move their aged inventory with a solid, prepared buyer, and whether the listing agent representing the sale has an above-average success rate. This is where the rubber meets the road and where the buyer's expert real estate broker needs to shine.

Though it may sound cliché, buyers still need to compile a comprehensive list of "pros and cons" important to their process. Literally, buyers should pull out a piece of paper and draw a line down the center. They should be asking themselves, "what is important about X & Y," defining what qualities they absolutely cannot live without, followed by secondary and tertiary needs, separating these from "pie-in-the-sky" features that would normally be seen on an episode of MTV Cribs, which—at the end of the day—can be tossed out of the equation.

In general, things to consider should include: affordability, location, property type, square footage, bedroom and bathroom count, lot type, nearby schooling, commute time, modern conveniences, and historic resale values. Of course, there are many more variables, but the aforementioned considerations are a good place to start.

During the offer process, a buyer should make sure the real estate broker researches comparable sales in the nearby area—typically within ½ mile for urban settings, 1 mile for suburban settings, and 3 miles for rural settings—all from within the past 6 months. Any sales beyond these distance parameters are probably not truly comparable, and any data beyond six months is too old to be relevant to the current market.

Though it is a sad necessity, buyers must mention the critical importance that all comparable sales are disclosed to them. The savvy buyer should be careful of the report that cherry-picks comparable sales to support the contract price. The picture presented to the buyer should be comprehensive, including the good, the bad, and the ugly in order to yield an educated and informed decision.

It is important for buyers to be careful when sellers and listing agents start saying things like, "it recently appraised for $x," or "the fair market value is $x." Buyers would be advised to isolate themselves from this emotional trap, as an appraisal is a backward-looking or "historic" tool that measures past sales and does not necessarily portray the true direction or velocity of the market.

At present, most markets have been and will continue in a negative or double-dip trajectory for months to come, making the usefulness of appraisals especially suspect. A professional real estate agent should perform a BPO or Broker's Price Opinion (if they don't know what a BPO is, run fast) to provide a forward-looking perspective of where the market is headed.

Also, fair market value is defined by what someone is willing to pay for a home. If no one has shown interest in the home (i.e. as defined by extended days-on-market or multiple price reductions), there is an obvious disconnect between seller and buyer and the fair market value is over-stated in the current list price.

In the end, buyers need to remember that purchasing real estate is a process of compromises. This fact becomes even more pronounced and obvious if multiple buyers are involved, such as spouses, investor partners, friends "going in" on a vacation home together, etc.

The most important thing for a buyer to remember is that there is no such thing as a perfect home. If you approach the process with realistic expectations and proper education, you stand a good chance at being successful in your search.

About The Author

Chase Horner

Horner Baker Partners
111 Village Pkwy, Bldg 2, Ste 201
Marietta, GA 30067

(770) 579-4060

chase@hornerbakerpartners.com

www.hornerbakerpartners.com

Passion, energy and focus—these are the tenets with which Chase Horner runs his business. As the Principal Broker of both Horner Baker Partners Real Estate and Southern Foreclosure–The REO Company in Atlanta, GA, Chase diligently oversees all aspects of each brokerage.

He is a long-time member of the Craig Proctor Real Estate Coaching Program—one of the nation's most successful networks of brokers, and an active member of the *National REO Brokers Association.* Over the course of his career, Chase has directed hundreds of successful real estate transactions. An alumnus of Emory University, Chase lives in Atlanta with his wife Dena and his Frisbee dog, Marshall.

10

Avoiding Buyer Mistakes

Bruce Hammer
Golden State Realty Group
Sacramento, California

The purchase and sale of real estate occurs around the United States, North America and all over the world every single day. Constantly, willing buyers are forming agreements with willing sellers to purchase homes. Considering the sheer number of people buying and selling, it may appear that the process is not overly complicated. But, in reality, it takes a lot of dedicated people, working together, to get someone from interested house hunter to home owner.

During this process, the buyer will be led down a road that has many possible places to take a "wrong turn." In most cases, they will have a real estate agent to guide them and keep them on the right road; and the better their real estate agent is at their job, the better the guidance. A big part of an agent's job is to minimize, if not eliminate, the "wrong turns" of buyer mistakes. In this chapter, a few of the more common and costly buyer mistakes have been summarized.

Purchasing Without an Understanding of Budget

In the beginning of the home-buying process, most real estate professionals will point their clients toward a mortgage loan officer to go through the pre-approval process. Obtaining a pre-approval letter from a lender is necessary because most home sellers will require one with any offer submitted.

Home sellers do not want to tie up their property with a buyer that isn't qualified to get a loan or complete the purchase. Until recently, anyone with something resembling a heartbeat could get a home loan. In recent years, however, the real estate market began to experience problems and mortgage lenders have tightened up the standards and qualifications for home buyers to finance their purchases.

Now, in order to get their pre-approval letter, buyers have to provide bank statements, tax returns and other documents to prove they earn what they claim to earn. While these new restrictions will preclude many from qualifying for pre-approval, the good news is that many will be spared the heartache of losing their homes to foreclosure or a forced short sale.

Most mortgage loan professionals will attempt to pre-approve a potential home buyer for the maximum amount of loan they can afford. This gives buyers more options in their home search. If a buyer knows they can successfully get a loan to purchase a $250,000 home, they also have the option of looking at homes anywhere below $250,000. It depends on the size of monthly payments that the buyer can handle.

Buyers should be aware that each lender has approval and underwriting guidelines that are based on several factors. They consider the amount of long-term vs. short-term debt the buyer and their family is managing. They consider length of employment, credit history, credit score, and several other factors. Unfortunately, while they are making decisions on an individual, the buyer's loan qualification is based on guidelines and computer models established for the "average person," and not a specific buyer.

Based on underwriting guidelines, a buyer may be able to afford a $250,000 home and easily make the monthly payments. However, at that price, they may find their finances stressed beyond their comfort level. What good is it to buy a wonderful new home if the monthly payment causes economic hardship?

When a home buyer gets a pre-approval letter, they should take a moment to review what their monthly payment will be, basing their review on the maximum amount in the pre-approved loan. In determining their monthly payments, they should be careful to consider property taxes, HOA dues (if any), and homeowner's insurance.

Additionally, they should speak to a qualified tax professional who can factor in deductible interest and property taxes which may show that the buyer can decrease their payroll tax withholdings to increase their take-home pay – one of the great benefits of home ownership! The bottom line here is that home buyers should get some assistance in calculating the approximate total monthly expense of home ownership before they write their offer.

One necessary side note to this relates to the actual pre-approval letter or document provided by the lender. In many cases, a buyer's offer to a seller may be lower than the amount they are approved to purchase. If a buyer is approved to purchase a $250,000 home, but only offers $240,000 to the seller, it's not in the buyer's best interest to disclose that they are approved for the higher amount. If the seller knows they are already approved for $250,000, they might be more likely to make a counter-offer for that higher amount.

Once the buyer possesses a pre-approval letter, they will know the maximum amount for which they can get a loan. They simply need to make an educated decision of how much they are willing to "afford" to purchase. Once this is determined, the future happy homeowners can begin their house hunting adventure.

Failing to Get a Home Inspection

On television crime dramas, a violent crime will be sometimes referred to as, "one committed in the heat of passion." In real estate purchases, buyers can get so caught up in the process of finding and negotiating for the right home, that they get blinded by "passion." While there is no violence involved, there is a "crime" in the sense that there could be damages to their financial future.

Whether buying a brand new or re-sale home, a real estate agent should be recommending a home inspection and the buyer should be listening to that recommendation. In truth, sometimes sellers forget to disclose things that they may or may not know about the home and its condition. In most states, home sellers are required by law to disclose known property defects, but the law cannot guarantee that sellers will know all possible defects.

It is best to think of an independent home inspection as the great equalizer that helps uncover defects and ensure buyers are as informed as possible about the condition of their future dream home. Typically, home inspections range in price from about $200 to $500. This expense at the beginning of the home purchase process could save a buyer tens of thousands of dollars down the road; well worth the relatively modest expense for ensuring the dream home being purchased today remains a dream home.

Compromising on Home Features

Ideally, when shopping for a home, the buyer should be thinking about the specific requirements they need or want to find in their dream home. Typically, they might consider size requirements, the number of bedrooms and bathrooms, proximity to work or school, quality of the local school district, and countless other features.

Some real estate markets might make it easier to check off all the "needs" or "wants" on the buyers wish list; other markets can be more challenging. In a seller's market (one where there are more buyers than available desirable homes); it may be difficult locating a home that meets the buyer's requirements simply because there is more competition for the same limited supply of homes.

Likewise, in a buyer's market (one where there are too many available homes for a smaller number of qualified buyers) larger inventory may translate to more choices that meet the buyer's criteria.

According to the National Association of Realtors®, people will, on average, spend about seven years in a home they purchase. Buyers who compromise on their desired home features could end up living through those seven years as if they were a prison sentence.

CHAPTER 10 – AVOIDING BUYER MISTAKES

It is important for a home buyer to think about these home features in terms of whether they are "needed" or merely "wanted." If a family of two adults and five children are shopping for a home, having four or five bedrooms may be considered a "need." Whereas, a couple with no children might "want" an extra room to use as a home office or study – but it isn't necessarily needed or required by them.

Breaking things down to what is "needed" vs. "wanted" can be helpful when discussing what the buyer can afford. Some of the dozens of topics or features a buyer may want to think about before making an offer might include:

- How many bedrooms, bathrooms, and total square footage are needed? This should be well thought-out and not a spur-of-the-moment decision. Does the buyer plan on starting a family (or adding to it)? Will they need an extra bedroom or bath? If buying with a spouse or significant other, both should make sure they agree on these needs.

- Is the home in the right location with easy access to streets, freeways, schools, parks, and local businesses? Is this important to the buyer? If so, they should visit their top areas of choice to ensure that these important needs are met.

- How far is the commute to work going to be? Sitting in stop-and-go freeway traffic for an hour each way may not be a problem – but it could be something to consider.

Besides finding a home with the required features, there needs to be some realistic balance between the buyer wants and desires and their financial ability and basic needs. A first-time buyer with a modest nest egg saved for their down payment and closing costs may be forced to compromise on their wish list.

If their situation only allows for the purchase of a home at a price up to $100,000 in an area where single family homes start at $150,000, they may be forced to consider something smaller. Likewise, maybe they can afford a single family home, but only in a price range that would get them into a "fixer," a home that requires numerous repairs and updates.

In summary, it is critical to make every effort to find a home with as many desired features as possible. At the same time, it is necessary to recognize that there could be limitations based on financial ability, geographic location, and supply and demand.

The bottom line is that buyers should consider all of the factors (both good and bad) and make an educated decision based on those factors before having their agent write their purchase offer.

Choosing an Inexperienced Sales Agent or Broker

All professionals, whether lawyers, physicians, insurance or real estate agents are generally required to take some education or college coursework. Some require college degrees, post-graduate and continuing education. Most are required to also pass a state-administered examination. But, with the exception of physicians, none are required to have someone supervise them in the field to ensure they know what they are doing after passing a state examination.

In the real estate industry, a licensed salesperson will generally have to hang their license under a broker who is supposed to "supervise" their activities. In truth, though, most brokers will simply offer training classes with hardly any checks and balances to ensure that the salespersons attend those classes.

There are national real estate organizations that have made great strides to increase educational opportunities and help reinforce best practices and higher levels of ethics amongst their members. But, just because an agent gets their license today and joins an association of other real estate agents tomorrow – doesn't necessarily mean that they are any more qualified or knowledgeable than another agent who chose not to join. So, what does this mean to the consumer looking for an agent to help them find and purchase a new home?

It's probably not the best idea to use cousin Vinnie who has never written a sales contract to help find the home, negotiate the price, and close the deal. An inexperienced agent may draft a purchase offer that commits the buyer to pay for items that, by local custom, are normally paid for by the seller. Likewise, an inexperienced agent may not know or understand inspection and financing contingencies – which could ultimately cost the buyer the home and/or forfeiture of their earnest money deposit.

ANSWERS FROM EXPERTS ON BUYING A HOME

Home buyers are literally making one of the largest single purchases in their lifetime – why shouldn't they find the most qualified person available to represent them? They should interview their prospective sales agent just like an employer would interview an employee for a job.

What kind of interview questions should be asked of a prospective real estate agent (buyer's representative)? Some recommended questions are:

- How many real estate sales have you personally closed over the last 12 months? (Ask for a printout from the Multiple Listing Service - this should be easy for the agent to provide).

- Is selling real estate your only job? Part-time real estate agents may not have the time to devote to you or your transaction. What if they work at their non-real estate job from 9AM to 5:30PM and cannot let an appraiser into a home, meet a home inspector, or allow a buyer access for a final walk-through?

- Are you currently involved in any litigation over a transaction you were associated with?

- Do you work alone, or are you supported by a team? Real estate agents who run their business as a team usually out-perform agents who work on their own because teams can generally provide superior customer service to their clients.

- Do you offer a "performance guarantee?" In other words, is the agent confident enough in their negotiation skills and abilities to back up their claims with a monetary penalty (payable to the buyer) if they don't perform? A typical guarantee might be, "I will save you at least $5,000 on the purchase price of your next home or I will pay you $1,000."

The bottom line is that with a purchase as large as a home, a buyer should be a discriminating consumer. They should ask hard questions. If the agent isn't convincing, doesn't have the right answers, or they just don't feel like they would be a good fit, then move on to the next "applicant." There are plenty of experienced, competent, and ethical agents to choose from; why take a chance using one with no experience? There is just too much at stake to go with an agent that is simply "adequate."

These are just a few of the many mistakes a buyer can make when they don't have the benefit of a great sales professional providing advice and helping them navigate that road from interested home buyer to homeowner. There are many more that can pop up from time to time. The buyer should remember to seek the right help, trust their advice, and ask the tough questions.

About The Author

Bruce Hammer

Golden State Realty Group
3835 N Freeway Blvd. Suite 140
Sacramento, CA 95834

(916) 960-1774

bruce@colemanhammer.com

www.sacramentohousefinder.com

Bruce Hammer was born and raised in the San Francisco Bay Area. After military service, he earned a BS degree from the College of Notre Dame in 1991 and an MBA in 1998. He got his real estate license in 1988 and began managing foreclosures in the loan servicing industry. He acquired, rehabbed, and sold foreclosed properties as an Asset Manager for PMI Mortgage Insurance Company. It was a natural progression to sell traditional and REO listings.

Bruce is co-owner of Golden State Realty Group, Inc., in Sacramento, CA. Bruce's strong work ethic and knowledge of the industry have earned him numerous industry awards and he is consistently ranked in the elite top one half of one percent of all practicing licensees in the Sacramento tri-county area.

Bruce is a member of the National REO Brokers Association, a Certified Distressed Property Expert, Life Member of the Sacramento Association of Realtors® Masters Club, and REO4Kids, a national organization of real estate brokers who support children's charities on every sale.

11

Finding the Best Deal

Aaron Kinn
Kinn Real Estate
Keller, Texas

ANSWERS FROM EXPERTS ON BUYING A HOME

One question on the mind of every buyer is, "How can I find the best deal when buying a home?" Everyone wants the best deal, whether they are buying real estate or anything else. Why is the term, "sale" used so much in marketing? Because to most people, sale means <u>deal</u>, and a *deal* is exactly what every person is looking for. Home buyers are no different.

Trouble can arise, however, when buyers try to figure out how to find a good real estate deal, how to maximize the deal, and how to determine that it actually is a deal when it is all said and done.

Let's start with the definition of a deal. Every individual buyer has a different take on what a deal means, but the term is almost always associated with getting a great price on an item. So, does a buyer think they got a deal just because they got a great price? Sometimes a perceived deal on the price is not much of a deal at all!

Imagine that a buyer purchased a home for $20,000 below its current market value, but the market has fallen at a rate of 5% per month for the past six months. Is this really a deal? It won't take long for the market's negative slide to catch up with that $20,000 savings.

That same example would also not constitute a deal if the buyer had to put twenty thousand dollars or more into the property in order to make it comparable to the other homes on the market. This is why the term deal has many hidden meanings.

When talking about price, the buyer needs to see the whole picture—this is where a good real estate agent comes in. A good real estate agent can provide a "comparative market analysis" (CMA) on the home to determine the market value of comparable properties in the same neighborhood.

Most people associate a CMA with home sellers, but a CMA can have equal, if not more importance for the home buyer. Unfortunately, many real estate agents don't perform a CMA when working with a buyer.

For example, if a home is priced at $200,000 and the buyer is interested in this home, many real estate agents will write an offer without researching the market. Without research, or doing a proper CMA, how is a buyer supposed to know if the home they are buying is a good deal? Unfortunately, this happens all too often and a buyer can end up offering more than they have to.

Even if the buyer feels that they got a great deal, a little research may indicate that the falling market turned their so-called deal into an over-payment. As illustrated here, a CMA is an absolute must when buying any home.

It is important that a CMA be done properly. Most real estate agents will only do a surface CMA of the property. They look at the home's square footage and number of bedrooms and bathrooms and then print a list of all homes in the same neighborhood listed for sale and sold in the past six months.

ANSWERS FROM EXPERTS ON BUYING A HOME

Is this really enough information? No! There are many other factors that need to be considered. The buyer needs to know many other things, such as whether the sellers paid closing costs on behalf of the buyers. This will better determine the net dollar amount properties are selling for in the area.

Is it enough to look at just the neighborhood? No! Some neighborhoods are very small, or have very little turnover. A radius search of at least one mile in every direction is recommended to find all sales that are comparable to the subject property.

How should these homes compare? In addition to having the same number of bathrooms and bedrooms, the homes should not be more than 15% larger or smaller than the subject property and no more than five years apart in age.

A professional agent will also obtain the "absorption rate" of the neighborhood and the comparable properties. The absorption rate tells the buyer how quickly or how slowly a market is moving. Although it sounds fancy, the absorption rate is nothing more than the number of homes being sold each month divided by the number of homes available for sale.

For example, if 100 homes are available for sale and only 5 homes sell each month, the absorption rate is 5%, which means there are 20 months of available inventory on the market. This doesn't account for the future inventory that is likely to hit the market. This is a key piece of information to know if you are a buyer trying to get a good deal.

Taking this a step further, the professional agent should also provide the success rate of sale of the comparable properties. Basically, this shows every home that has been on the market in the past six months and every property that has sold as well.

For example, if there have been 150 homes on the market for sale—including active properties, properties under contract, those that have expired, and those that have sold—and only 20 of these were sold in the past six months, this would be a successful selling rate of only 13%. This rate will help to determine the price at which a particular home should sell, and also help the buyer in determining a good initial offer to make on the home. All of these factors need to be used in order to determine how much to offer.

So far, the focus has been on determining a good deal with regard to price. There are many other factors, however, that determine whether or not a home is a good deal. These factors have to do with a buyer's personal preferences. Homes may be situated in a specific neighborhood or school district or have amenities that no other home can match.

The importance of these factors will vary from buyer to buyer, and will influence the buyer's offer. Overall, though, home buying usually comes down to price, and few homes can offer a better price than foreclosed homes.

When talking about foreclosures, it is important to understand a few key terms. Put simply, a foreclosure is a home for which the owner has stopped making payments, causing the bank to put it up for auction.

Many in real estate refer to a home as a foreclosure when trying to sell it for a bank or financial institution. This is actually more correctly referred to as an REO property (Real Estate Owned, by the bank).

Why are these homes often the first that are sought out by many buyers? It is simply a perception that these homes are a great deal. Truly, they often are, and every buyer should consider them. Often, they are priced less than other comparable properties in the same area.

The reason for the discount is often times these properties need some sort of work or updating in order to get them to the standards of other comparable properties. Most of these homes are sold "as-is," meaning that the bank will do no work on the property, no matter what is found on an inspection report. This is why there is usually a monetary reward, or a lower price, on a bank-owned home than what you typically find on any other property available on the market.

Another type of home that represents a good deal to the buyer is the "short sale." A short sale home is where the property owner owes more than the home is worth. The property owner may be delinquent in their payments due to a hardship of some type, like a divorce, job loss, death in the family, or any other situation.

The bank will review the owner's financials in great detail, then weigh the outcome of accepting an offer "short" of what is owed versus foreclosing on the home owner and selling the home as an REO property. Banks may be willing to accept less than is owed because of the tremendous cost of securing, marketing, preserving, and selling the REO property.

Often, short sales can represent an even better deal to the buyer than REO properties because many of the extra costs incurred by the bank on an REO property are avoided with a short sale. Typically, the owner is still living in the property and maintaining it so the bank doesn't have to.

Still, the extensive report and financial calculations by the banks and their loss mitigators are not without drawbacks. The biggest drawback is the overall time it takes to complete these sales. If the buyer is in no hurry to move into their home, or to even get an answer on their offer in a reasonable period of time, then the short sale can be the perfect option.

It typically takes anywhere from two months to as many as eight months to even get an answer on whether the buyer's offer is acceptable. The other big drawback is that like REO properties, the buyer must purchase the home "as-is".

In both the case of the short sale and the REO, it is imperative for the real estate agent to do their homework on repair issues, and other costs that could tip the scales on whether or not the purchase is a great deal for their client.

Other sources for finding great deals are readily available to anybody with an Internet connection. The MLS (Multiple Listing Service) or affiliated websites like Realtor.com provide every listing available for sale in the local MLS where sellers have hired an agent. Often, this includes all short sales, REOs, distress sales, investor sales, and many other types of properties that can represent a good deal for the buyer.

One market segment that is often overlooked by many buyers and their real estate agents is off-market inventory. Off-market inventory is often referred to by real estate agents as expired, canceled or withdrawn listings. In other words, these sellers were trying to sell their home, but for some reason, the home did not sell.

The mindset of the buyer has to be one of catching these people in a vulnerable state. Most likely, they have been on the market for a minimum of four to six months, and within that time frame have had many strangers disturbing their normal routine and walking through their home and looking through their things.

These off-market sellers are frustrated that no one has decided to purchase their home. In most cases, a savvy real estate agent can pull up all the details on these properties and send them to their buyers. They can also gather contact information for these sellers and set up a private showing with the potential buyer.

This benefits the buyer looking for a deal because the seller will probably be more willing to negotiate a lower price on the home because it is a one-on-one situation. The buyer solves their problem, and they will no longer have anyone else walking through their home.

In this situation, the seller can afford to sell their home for less than it was previously listed because they now only have to pay one agent; the agent representing the buyer. Due to this savings, they are usually willing to cut their price considerably and the buyer inherits the savings that were once reserved for paying commission.

No matter how the house is found, whether a foreclosure, REO, short sale, off-market home, traditional seller, or any other type of home, the key component to make everything work effectively for the home buyer is a top notch real estate agent working on their behalf.

The difference in working with an average agent and an exceptional agent can be the difference in getting a good deal or no deal. Often, if a buyer chooses to work with an average agent, they will not get as good of a deal as they would if they had chosen a better agent.

About The Author

Aaron Kinn

Kinn Real Estate
1668 Keller Parkway, Suite 400
Keller, TX 76248

(817) 380-5610

aaron@aaronkinn.com

www.aaronkinn.com

Aaron Kinn is a Texas real estate broker, licensed for nearly ten years. Aaron and his business partners sell real estate in Dallas, Tarrant, Denton, Johnson, Ellis, Hood, Parker, and Wise counties in Texas. Over the past ten years, Aaron has helped over 1,000 people achieve the American dream.

Born in Rochelle, Illinois, Aaron attended Monmouth College where he obtained a Bachelor of Arts degree in 1998. After graduating college, Aaron become a High School Art teacher. He coached baseball and basketball for four years until he discovered his passion for real estate.

After starting his real estate career as the Rookie of the Year, Aaron became a top producer among the 50 agents at his company. He is ranked in the top 1% of agents in the Dallas/Fort Worth area and believes in giving back to the community. He belongs to REO4Kids, a national group whose members give $100 to children's charities for every home sold. Aaron's biggest passion for the past five years is being the best dad that he can be to his only daughter, Eva!

12

Buying A Foreclosed Home

Lester Cox

Pacific Arizona Real Estate
Tempe, Arizona

Buying a foreclosed home can be a great way to get a great deal on a home, and, in some instances, the buyer can literally save tens of thousands of dollars. Known in the real estate world as a "Real Estate Owned," REO properties are unlike any other type of purchase, and definitely not real estate the old-fashioned way.

First of all, it is important to understand who the players are. Often that is hard to determine. It is also important to understand that in the past, many mortgages were placed in a pool of loans, packaged into security instruments, and sold to various investors.

Because of this, the mortgage on a home may be owned by multiple individuals or principles, and it is possible that none of the parties know each other—they could even be in different countries. This can be one reason for long delays in getting offers approved and getting the final details completed on closing documents.

In traditional real estate, a buyer will simply look at different homes and upon finding the right one, use an agent to complete the transaction. However, when hunting for a good deal on an REO property, it is very important to find an agent who is experienced in working specifically with the REO purchasing process, as these properties represent a highly specialized industry.

In the past, most agents specializing in REO simply worked with the *seller* of the property, and the buyer would use any agent to make the purchase. But now, many well-known REO agencies have created specialized departments to assist buyers. These agents may have some access to the REO department where they can get insider information on the "owners" of the REO property.

Many prospective buyers have a friend or relative in the real estate business. If that friend or relative does not have REO buyer experience, it would be wise to have them give a referral to an agent who does. The buyer will get a great deal and a knowledgeable agent, and the friend or relative will get a referral fee for passing the name along to a capable agent—everyone wins.

To begin, it is helpful for the buyer to start with a list of things that he or she can do to get the best possible home at the best possible price.

Almost all sellers of REO properties require pre-approval when a loan is required to complete the purchase. Additionally, the seller may have specific lenders with whom the buyer must qualify. This gives the seller assurance that the buyer is qualified to make the purchase and that this qualification has been provided by a source they deem to be reliable.

For a prospective buyer, there is no risk that having their credit score pulled multiple times will hurt their credit score—this rule, which applies to home buying, was established specifically to prevent predatory lending. While a buyer may feel justified in complaining about this process, they should be assured that it is not an unreasonable request.

The seller is probably going to be taking a significant loss on the property and for every passing month that they own the property, it costs them more money. As a result, the seller needs to know that the buyer can qualify for a loan to pay for the home. There is really no reason for the buyer to resist pre-approval with the seller's pre-determined lender—it makes the entire process easier for all parties. Refusal on the part of the buyer could result in another refusal—a refusal from the seller to sell the home to the uncooperative buyer.

The buyer should do their due diligence up front. REO homes are always sold "as-is", meaning that the seller is not required to perform any repairs on the property. As such, this burden falls on the buyer. Fortunately, most state purchase agreements allow a buyer a specified time frame in which to perform inspections.

A diligent buyer will conduct their investigation work prior to placing an offer. By doing this investigation up front, and hopefully shortening the purchase agreement's time frame for inspections, the buyer can state, in the contract, that they have inspected the property thoroughly and do not anticipate requesting any repairs. In effect, they are informing the seller that the condition of the property is already considered in the offering price.

The escrow closing date is when the buyer takes possession and ownership of the property. When dealing with foreclosed homes, the closing date may not always occur on the exact date of the original agreement.

The bank seller expects the closing to fall on the agreed-upon date and if the buyers are unable to close on time, they may be required to pay a penalty to the seller for extending the closing. If however, the delay is not the fault of the buyer, no penalty is charged to the buyer, but the seller does not pay a penalty either.

Additionally, asset managers garner much of their compensation for closing a certain number of transactions each month. This "bonus system" makes up a good part of their overall compensation package, so they are sensitive to getting a certain number of transactions closed in a month.

Most asset managers will not allow the loss of a bonus to affect the outcome of the transaction, but if all things are equal on the initial offer, and your closing date allows the asset manager to receive a bonus for that month, the buyer stands a much better chance of having their offer selected.

The asset manager may be handling as many as three or four hundred files at a time, potentially in different areas of the country with different local customs and ordinances. In spite of these potential sources of delay, the buyer should remain patient and flexible. The buyer must remember that generally, the seller of a foreclosed home is taking a substantial loss and the buyer is probably getting a very, very good deal.

The massive savings represented in the purchase of a foreclosed home should more than compensate for the aforementioned inconveniences.

Diligence should be matched with prudence, and it is very prudent to learn about the local real-estate market and confirm that your agent also has a good understanding of the local market. In all markets, there are many publicly available statistics that can tell a buyer how much a home is worth and the amount they should offer to purchase it.

Some of these statistics include the number of days it typically takes for a home to sell in the local market, as well as the average ratio between sale price and asking price. These statistics can tell a buyer how many homes are selling each month, how many homes are entering the market each month, and these numbers can be filtered to show only specific locations and property types.

This is all highly important information for the prospective buyer, and it is data that a good agent will know and make available to the buyer. If the agent cannot supply such data, the buyer should look for a new agent.

When you've found the right home and are ready to write an offer, ask your agent to contact the listing agent to determine whether other offers have already been made on the property and if more offers are expected.

The agent should inquire about what the buyer can add to their offer to make it more attractive to the asset manager — items such as earnest money, closing dates, title companies, etc. As already mentioned, the buyer should be pre-approved with the specific lender the seller has requested. This allows the seller an opportunity to recoup some of their loss by having their own company provide the new loan.

Again, this is often the area of biggest complaint for the buyer, but it doesn't change the fact that if the buyer is serious about purchasing the home, he or she should comply with the wishes of the seller. The buyer shouldn't just comply with these wishes, but go above and beyond them by seeking a full-blown loan qualification. This can provide additional information to the seller which will make the buyer's offer stand out from the others.

When the buyer has received pre-approval or better yet, a full-blown approval, it is time to determine the offering price by comparing the property being sold to anything else on the market. With these steps taken, the buyer should then aim for a closing date in about thirty days. If the buyer will be paying cash, there will be no need for loan approval, only proof that the buyer indeed possesses the available funds to complete the transaction.

For example, if the cash buyer is writing an offer on the third day of the month, he or she could set the closing date to the twenty-fifth day of the month. Such a time frame would still leave plenty of room for inspections, and makes the closing date soon enough to give the asset manager a chance at a bonus. Typically, closing dates that fall at the very end of the month are susceptible to snafus, so they should be avoided.

For the buyer, it is important that they understand what "net" means to the seller. The seller will be looking at how much money they have after expenses, repairs, allowances, closing costs, etc. have been paid. If the buyer needs closing cost assistance, they should never request more than the absolute minimum needed for the lender to complete the transaction, and they should only make this request if they are already putting down an amount equal to a loan-to-value benchmark.

For example, if the buyer can only afford to put down 20% on a $200,000 sale and the closing costs are anticipated to run around $5,000, then the buyer should ask for $5,000 toward closing cost assistance.

But, if the buyer can afford a higher down payment, such as $60,000 on a $200,000 sale, then it would be wise to lower the down payment (to $55,000, for example) and pay the closing costs out of pocket while reducing the offer price to $195,000. A buyer who is able to pay their own closing costs is going to make the seller happy and, in most cases, is making a smart financial decision for themselves.

After the price and closing date have been selected and the seller's preferred lender has issued an approval, buyer should fully intend on using that lender as well as the seller's preferred title company. Although the buyer can choose another lender and title company, in most cases, the title insurance has already been purchased by the seller and the "seller-preferred" lender may offer attractive perks to secure their business. Since there are only a few writers of title insurance policies, it makes little difference which title company that might be.

The buyer should simply take the path of least resistance and use the closing company or attorney the seller has selected. The buyer should limit the inspection period as much as possible and understand what "as-is" means. The buyer is obtaining the property as it sits today, so if they are serious about getting their offer accepted, he or she should inform the seller that they are aware of any problems with the property—such as a missing water heater, worn out carpets, cracked tiles in a bathroom, etc.

The buyer should be making their offer with any such issues already taken into consideration and should not ask the seller for any repairs or allowances for repairs. The buyer must understand that the seller has no information on the home and will not sign any disclosures.

The buyer should ask their agent to explain the types of things that would be disclosed if the seller were making a disclosure. The buyer should then conduct their own investigation on any items of importance. Typically, there is a standard form that a buyer can review to learn about the items normally disclosed by a seller.

If the minimum earnest money is $1,000 and the buyer can put down $10,000, the buyer should make the earnest money a more substantial amount. Remember, it's called "earnest" money and from the perspective of the seller, a larger amount certainly seems more "earnest."

The buyer should be certain that all parties understand and agree to the contract timeline and know when the earnest money will no longer be refundable. If a buyer misses the inspection period deadline or the closing date, they should not expect to get their earnest money back—it just doesn't work that way. Remember, the higher the selling price, the higher the earnest money should be.

To summarize, the best strategies for a buyer are:

- Make a good and well-informed offer up front with reference to earnest money and inspection timeline.

- Don't request excessive sums of money for closing costs

- Shoot for a realistic closing date that offers the asset manager the best chance at receiving a bonus

- Have a firm understanding of what "as-is" means by fully taking into account the present condition of the home and absorbing that into the offer price

- Allow for a serious earnest money deposit, keep inspection periods at a minimum, and be mindful of the "net" amount the seller will receive

- Above all, remember that you should be getting a very good bargain on the home; be flexible, but also diligent

About The Author

Lester Cox

Pacific Arizona Realty
5440 S Lakeshore #104
Tempe, AZ 85283

(480) 775-7700

lester@wesellaz.com

www.wesellaz.com

Lester Cox was born and raised in the mid-western part of the country, Kansas City, MO. His father was a respected local businessman who passed along his strong work ethic and the belief that there is no ceiling on what is possible.

When he was 17, Lester relocated to Phoenix with his mother and younger sister after the death of his father. After high school, Lester attended Phoenix College and Arizona State University where he studied business. After serving four years in the United States Air Force, Lester entered the real estate arena where he has found great success for more than 40 years.

His experience includes residential sales, new home sales, commercial real estate, development, and home building. In 1995, he founded his own company and began building a real estate team in 2001. To date, Lester has been responsible for over 5,000 successful transaction totaling more than a *billion dollars* in sales.

He and his team consistently close 400 to 500+ transactions each year and Lester has received numerous awards and accolades as one of the top real estate agents in Arizona and the real estate industry.

Lester is active in his community, giving thousands of dollars each year to charities benefitting children, like Make-A-Wish Foundation and Boys and Girls Clubs of America. He currently serves on the Board of Directors for REO4Kids, National Association of Hispanic Real Estate Professionals, and is a founding member of three real estate mastermind groups.

Lester is also a professional real estate coach for the Craig Proctor coaching program and co-facilitator of the Diamond Mastermind Group. He is the Master Broker for Arizona for the National REO Brokers Association.

Lester and his wife Pat have been married for 37 years and both work in their real estate company. They reside in Chandler, Arizona, with their Boxer named Lindlee and a Papillion named Trixie. They enjoy spending time with their siblings, many nieces and nephews, and close friends.

13

Getting A Good Deal

Warren Flax

Platinum Realty Team
Langhorne, Pennsylvania

ANSWERS FROM EXPERTS ON BUYING A HOME

If the late-night TV blowhards and Internet gurus have taught the world anything, it is that tons of motivated sellers are just dying to give away their homes for prices as low as 30% of their current market value. But is that true?

Here's a question: even if a home could be bought for such a low price, would a buyer even want it? If someone offered a buyer a house in an area where they didn't want to live, or they offered a house that was too small for the buyer's needs, would it matter that the home was being offered at a discount? Probably not.

Every week, people throw out hundreds of coupons that come in the mail offering tremendous deals on products they don't want or need. So, until a buyer can determine what they need in a home, they cannot know what a good deal looks like.

The best home, for any buyer, will be a combination of tradeoffs. However, there are four levers a buyer can pull to affect their search:

1.) Price
2.) Location
3.) Size
4.) Condition.

By looking carefully at these four criteria and matching them with their needs, a buyer can pinpoint a great deal on a home.

CHAPTER 13 – GETTING A GOOD DEAL

1) Price

Is cheapest the best? If it is, then all those Mercedes dealerships would never even exist. The same analogy can be applied to the real estate market—the best price for a buyer to pay for home is a combination of the other factors that make the home right for them, combined with the current market conditions. Is it worth some extra money to be in the school district that is best for your kids?

Can a buyer save money by getting a home that has dated furnishings like wallpaper, kitchen cabinets and bathroom tiles? Would they want to? Would they rather pay more for an extra bedroom or get a newer home that has one less bedroom? Every buyer's needs are unique, and every buyer needs to understand these needs in order to match themselves with the best deal.

First, a buyer needs to determine how much they can afford to spend. If the buyer needs a mortgage to purchase their home, then they are essentially buying a monthly payment. There are lots of different formulas used to determine the "right" monthly payment, but a general rule that most mortgage companies use is that the housing payment (the mortgage plus the property taxes and insurance) be no more than 28% to 31% of total gross income.

For example, Joe and Jane earn a combined $6,000 each month before taxes. Allocating 28% of their gross income would allow $1,680 per month toward a house payment which included principal, interest, taxes and insurance. This assumes that they don't have a lot of other debts.

If a borrower has other debts, banks also check the "back end ratio" to make sure that other debts don't make the house too risky of an investment. The maximum back end ratio allowed is usually between 36 and 41%. If Joe and Jane spend $600/month on car payments, $200/month on student loans and their lender is using a back-end ratio maximum of 40%, then the most they can borrow is $1,600/month (40% of $6,000 is $2,400, minus the $800 they are already spending on other debt each month).

2) Location

Yes, location is an important part of determining whether or not a buyer gets a good deal. No, it's not the only factor. The old cliché of "location, location, location" is unhelpful because, in any given market, the location of a home is only one factor that buyers consider and it's just as unchangeable as market conditions or size. For an in-depth discussion about how timing matters more than location, Robert Campbell's "Timing the Real Estate Market" is an informative read.

The best way to approach location is for the buyer to put down the laptop, turn off the cell phone, and get in the car and out into the world! As much as one can learn by searching the Internet and making phone calls, there is no substitute for getting out there and gaining first-hand knowledge. No one on earth can tell a buyer what is a "good" or "bad" neighborhood, because everyone feels differently in different settings.

Experienced real estate brokers can share dozens of stories about previous clients who felt uncomfortable in the most expensive neighborhoods as well as other buyers who felt quite comfortable in areas where the broker wanted to roll up the windows and slam on the gas pedal. At the end of the day, buyers need to determine the location that works best for them.

The most important thing a buyer can do is determine exactly where they want to own a home. Remember that due to fair housing laws, a real estate broker will not be able to share their personal opinion about neighborhoods or school districts.

It's up to the buyer to define this element of the home search on their own. Once this is done the entire search becomes easier, as a good real estate professional can help with showing the price range of homes available in the area. A good agent will also show exactly how the buyer can use the flexibility with size and condition to find the right home in their price range.

3) Size

At the risk of offending the men out there, it must be said that bigger is not always better. Just ask the folks who bought McMansions during the real estate boom how they feel now that the market has tanked. Many are paying inflated property taxes on homes that are now worth half of their purchase price.

The best sized home for a buyer is the size that will still be comfortable five to seven years later. One common mistake that first-time buyers make is settling for only a small increase in space from their current rental. Buyers need to consider what sort of space requirements they will have down the line, as well as today. Will an older relative need to move in 3 years from now? Will there be additional children?

Additional space in a home, such as basements, garages and attics that can be used for storage and closet space are critical components of making sure that the current purchase is still functional for the buyer years down the line. Paying a little extra today to prevent a second move in the near future could be the best money a buyer ever spends.

4) Condition

A home's condition might be the best opportunity for a buyer to save in the short term, provided that they are willing to educate themselves and put in some work. A company has made millions of dollars advertising that they buy ugly houses. This marketing slogan works well because the majority of buyers will pay a premium for pretty houses.

Buyers who are serious about saving money should try this: walk into a furnished house and picture it bare—forgetting the colors, the furniture, and the furnishings—and just fixate on the layout of the rooms and the ceiling height. It's pretty tough, isn't it?

On the day of closing, once the seller has moved out all of their items and cleaned the home, this is all that will remain and, for the most part, it's all stuff that the buyer can control. It's common for a house to sell for $20,000 or $30,000 less than the same house on the same side of the street, simply because it has wallpaper or carpeting that most buyers don't like. This is a great opportunity for buyers to save money.

CHAPTER 13 – GETTING A GOOD DEAL

When a buyer has found a home that meets their criteria, fits their price range, and feels better than all the other homes they have visited, they know they have a good deal. When the search is over and they've landed their dream home, they can take a deep breath, appreciate their accomplishment, and get some rest.

About The Author

Warren Flax

Platinum Realty Team
301 Oxford Valley Rd, Suite 201A
Yardley, PA 19067

(215) 945-3000

warren@prtemail.com

www.warrenflax.com

Warren Flax was born and raised in Philadelphia, PA, and graduated from Carnegie Mellon University. He earned a Masters degree from Wharton School and the Lauder Institute at the University of Pennsylvania. In 1991 he volunteered in Israel during the first Persian Gulf War and survived 39 Scud missile attacks while at a hospital base near Tel Aviv.

Upon returning home, Warren began anchoring and reporting television sports at stations in Bakersfield, CA, Ft. Myers, FL, and Seattle, WA. In 1998 he returned to Israel to volunteer while studying Hebrew and working on an agricultural kibbutz. He also worked in Tel Aviv translating and editing documents, including for then-defense Minister and eventual Prime Minister Ariel Sharon.

Warren moved to South America to study Spanish and work in his family's art material business. While there, he met and married his wife, Rocio. After the arrival of their children, Julia and Joshua, Warren became a real estate agent in 2004. He currently has offices in Pennsylvania and New Jersey.

14

Buying a For Sale by Owner

Joey Trombley
Kavanaugh Realty
Rouses Point, New York

ANSWERS FROM EXPERTS ON BUYING A HOME

Buying a home for most people is one of the most important and expensive purchases that they will make in their lifetime. I think you will agree that buying a home is a process, not an event. You just don't wake up one morning and say, "Honey lets go buy a home this morning." There are a lot of other factors involved.

What type of home do you want to buy? Do you want a one-story home or a two-story home or maybe a condo or town house? What area do you want to live in? Do you want a rural setting or a city setting? How much home can you afford? Do you talk to a lender first before looking at homes? Another question to ask yourself is should I buy a home using a real estate agent or try to buy a For Sale by Owner?

Let's first look at the dynamics of buying a For Sale by Owner. The main reason a home owner tries to sell a home themselves is because they want to avoid paying a commission. The main reason that a person would want to buy directly from an owner instead of using a real estate agent is because they want to save the commission. Do you see the dilemma?

Both parties want to save the commission but there is only one commission to save. There is a misconception that homes are cheaper if you buy directly from the owner because you don't have to pay a commission. The reality is a home is worth what it is worth in any given market regardless of whether there is a real estate agent involved.

CHAPTER 14 – BUYING A "FOR SALE BY OWNER"

A real estate commission is the cost of doing business if a real estate agent is involved. Let's take an in-depth look at both options:

Option A: Buying a Home Directly From the Owner

First off, you will be working directly with the seller. This can be good but can also be bad. The good part is that the seller will likely have a very thorough knowledge of the home. The bad part is you will have to negotiate directly with the seller and neither of you are good at it. This is not an easy thing to do. Buying or selling a home is a very emotional experience for both parties. Experience has shown that deals often fall apart because emotions get in the way.

You may feel that you will get a better deal because there is not a real estate agent involved. Remember, both parties want to save the real estate commission but there is only one commission to save. The only person that will save a commission is the seller because that is the fee they would pay if a real estate agent were to sell it for them. So no matter how much you pay for a home purchased directly from the seller you will not save the real estate commission. It can only be the seller who saves the commission.

You should be aware that your legal costs will be higher working directly with the seller because the real estate attorney or title company will have more work to do. Without a real estate agent being involved they will have to do the leg work that the real estate agent would have done for you.

Option B: Working With an Agent

The real estate agent will represent you as a buyer's agent. Their fiduciary responsibility is twofold:

1) help you secure the home of your dreams
2) help to negotiate the lowest purchase price possible

Your real estate agent will keep you up to date with the latest properties that match your home buying criteria. Instead of trying to sift through hundreds of homes, you only review the homes that have the amenities you are looking for.

In most markets these new listings will be sent to you within an hour of coming on the Multiple Listing Service (MLS). A buyers agent working for you will write the offer and ensure that the paperwork is complete, correct, and delivered to the appropriate parties such as your attorney, lender, and title company to name a few. All this will be done in a timely fashion because an experienced agent does it several times a month.

Ask an attorney or a title company whether they would prefer a purchase offer negotiated between a buyer and For Sale by Owner seller or a purchase offer negotiated between a buyer and seller with at least one real estate agent involved. The majority will tell you that they would prefer having an agent involved because transactions go more smoothly and close on time when an experienced agent is involved.

A real estate agent working for you will help you find a home, negotiate on your behalf, write the offer, and handle all of the paperwork required by the Title Company or attorney. Buyer's agents are paid by the listing agent from the proceeds of the sale and all of these services don't cost you a thing!

In closing, I will share another advantage of using a real estate agent to help you purchase the home of your dreams. We were recently working with a buyer who found a home that they absolutely loved. We were able to negotiate $30,000 dollars off the purchase price for them.

Over the life of a 30-year loan these homeowners are going to save approximately $60,000 dollars in payments. That is some serious money! Let's say a buyer's agent only saved you $10,000 dollars. That would be approximately $20,000 dollars over the life of the loan. When negotiating on a home, it makes sense to hire a professional, especially if someone else is paying the bill!

About The Author

Joey Trombley

Kavanaugh Realty
36 Champlain St
Rouses Point, NY 12979

(518) 572-0441

joey@joeytrombley.com

www.joeytrombley.com

Joey Trombley has been in the real estate business for 27 years. He's been the Broker/Owner of Kavanaugh Realty, nestled in upstate NY for the past 19 years.

Joey has been involved in Craig Proctor's Quantum Leap coaching for 13 years and has been coaching real estate agents in the program for the past 5 years. The Kavanaugh Realty team consistently outsells all other teams in the area and Joey's personal sales consistently rank in the top three individuals on the Real Estate Board.

Joey has been married for 26 years and has three children. Gaelan went to Plattsburgh State and currently works on the real estate team. Sagan is attending the State University in Albany, NY, and Maura is in high school.

15

Negotiating
The Purchase

Paul Rushforth
Paul Rushforth Real Estate
Ottawa, Ontario

Once the buyer has found a property that they wish to purchase, it's time for the real estate agent to really shine. Most people don't realize that, during the home-purchase process, most of the work done by the real estate agent is done behind the scenes—in the form of research, analysis, and preparation—well before the negotiation even begins.

The educated real estate agent will be familiar with pricing and market trends in the area, and will already have an idea about whether the asking price is in the right range, if it's high, or most urgently, if it is low. A low asking price will increase the likelihood of competing offers, so the negotiation strategy here will be different than a non-competitive situation, and time will clearly be of the essence.

To develop an appropriate negotiation strategy, it is critical to do a proper Comparative Market Analysis on the property in question, in order to determine a range for the fair market value of that property. Effectively, it's the same preparation that a real estate agent would do in order to arrive at a price when the property is listed. In a Comparative Market Analysis, many factors have to be considered in order to come up with a recommended price. Ideally, the data being considered will be for identical properties sold in the same neighborhood within a very recent time frame.

However, the reality is that typically, there will be some differences between the subject property and the sold properties that will require making adjustments to arrive at a final price. By looking closely at the sum of the recent comparable sales, current market conditions, as well as factoring in the required adjustments, an agent can educate the buyer about what the price range should be for the property.

Another factor that the buyer's agent needs to be aware of is how long the property stays on the market. If a house is fresh on the market, the seller will typically be less likely to negotiate the price. If a seller has a property on the market without an offer for quite some time, the buyer should take this into consideration and adjust their offer accordingly.

Now, the approach to negotiation will depend on the sum of the pricing relationship, the motivation of both parties, and whether or not there is a competing offer. At the end of the day, the key to successful negotiation is to reach a conclusion acceptable to both parties. This starts with effective communication between real estate agents. It has often been said that there is no substitute for good manners, and there will be no exception here.

Prior to preparing an offer on a property, take the time to call the listing agent to let them know about the intent to submit an offer. Find out when an offer presentation will be possible, or, better yet, if it is possible to make the offer presentation in person to the seller—especially critical in a multiple offer situation. Often, the buyer's agent may already have a good working relationship with the listing agent. However, as in any business relationship, treating the other party with manners and respect will go a lot further to help negotiations than being overly aggressive.

There is a great deal of information that a buyer's agent can obtain, just by asking the listing agent a few questions. Obviously, the call needs to be made to ensure that the property is still available for purchase. The buyer's real estate agent also needs to find out if there are other offers anticipated which might put their client in a competitive situation, thus requiring a different strategy.

Often, the buyer's real estate agent will be able to make some additional key determinations about the motivations of the seller by asking direct questions about the seller's preferences regarding the closing date. A seller looking for an immediate close may have another home to move to (and, more importantly, pay for), and thus would be more motivated to sell than someone not facing such requirements. If the buyer is able to accommodate a very specific closing date as requested by the seller, the buyer may be able to use that as leverage when negotiating the price.

Lastly, any fixtures or chattels (personal property) to be included in the offer should be discussed prior to submitting an offer, as they often become needless points of contention in a negotiation if they are not clarified from the start. It is important to first understand where the other side is coming from in order to determine the approach.

In a multiple-offer situation, the old expression of "you never have a second chance to make a first impression" is doubly true. Typically, the buyer will have only one attempt to put their best foot forward. This means that the offer with the best overall package will be successful. Closing dates and conditions (or lack thereof) will have a significant impact on a seller's decision, but the buyer should be prepared to make their top cash offer to the seller on the spot, as a counter offer opportunity is unlikely.

There are two key elements to a winning multiple-offer strategy. First, the seller's real estate agent should ask to present the offer in person—this way, the offer can be presented fairly and favorably, giving the chance to explain the offer and tell the seller a bit about the buyer, making it a more personal experience—it's harder to say no to a real person. Second, the buyer should be easily accessible (for example, waiting in the car outside the house) in case there are any questions that need to be addressed immediately. This also demonstrates that the buyer is serious. Unless there is a large discrepancy between offers, it is very rare to walk away from this situation without an accepted offer in hand for the buyer.

In a non-competitive situation, once the buyer's agent has the background work completed, it's time to begin the negotiation process. Maintaining a positive relationship with both the listing agent and the seller is critical for a successful negotiation. The actual negotiation can create a great deal of tension for both buyer and seller, as buying and selling a home involves a great deal of emotion and, of course, money.

The friendlier the approach, the more likely a deal will be able to be put together. Right from the beginning, it is important to let the listing agent know that the objective is to be fair, and to make a deal to which everyone can agree.

Since the proper preparation has been done in advance, there is an excellent chance that the negotiation will be successful, and that a middle ground can be reached between parties. In presenting the buyer's offer, the focus should be in presenting the position positively, and demonstrating fairness for both parties.

If there is a substantial difference between the asking price and the price offered, there should be evidence to support the buyer's decision to proceed at the lower price, in the interest of making a fair offer. Keeping this presentation to the seller positive rather than criticizing them will make the seller less defensive and more likely to consider the buyer's position, even in the absence of agreement. Additional relevant market data from the Comparative Market Analysis can also be used to establish evidence of a fair offer.

So, the initial offer has been presented, but things appear to be reaching a standstill. What might cause the process to enter a deadlock? In most cases, it will be about money; but sometimes other factors interfere as well. If there is more than one variable potentially affecting the outcome, it is important to isolate any objections in order to allow the negotiation to continue to progress.

In essence, if the objections can be identified and handled separately from the body of the offer, which is otherwise deemed acceptable to both parties, it will be significantly easier to reach a positive conclusion—a win-win for everyone. The ability to think creatively to find solutions that are mutually agreeable to both parties can be the difference between a successful negotiation and a dead deal. Sometimes, making a suggestion such as advancing a closing date (so that the seller won't have to carry the house expenses during that time) can have the same effect for the seller's bottom line as a price increase, resulting in an accepted offer.

This won't always mean convincing a seller to accept less money to reach an accepted offer—many times, this will mean reinforcing to the buyer the positive attributes of the property, enabling them to justify paying a little bit more for their dream house. Whether that value is strictly monetary or something less quantifiable, like the ability to spend more time with family due to a shorter commute or the proximity to a desirable school, it is up to the buyer's real estate agent to ensure that the buyer is considering all of the factors when making a decision in a negotiation.

It is still possible that, even after doing everything right during the negotiation process, the two parties just can't find common ground. It is important not to burn any bridges, but rather, be tactful and careful not to offend the other party. Both buyer and seller will be disappointed when a negotiation doesn't come together, but it is important to end on a friendly note in order to keep the door open for the possibility of a future negotiation—not only with that particular seller, but also for future negotiations with the other real estate agent. After all, reputation is critical in the real estate business, and it is easier to maintain a positive reputation than to repair a tarnished one. For the buyer's agent, it is far better to be remembered by all parties as a competent, respected professional—with or without a deal.

About The Author

Paul Rushforth

Paul Rushforth Real Estate
3002 St. Joseph Blvd
Ottawa, Ontario K1E 1E2

(613) 788-2122

information@paulrushforth.com

www.paulrushforth.com

Following a 10-year professional hockey career in North America and Europe as both a player and assistant coach, Paul decided to bring his enthusiasm, dedication and organizational skills to real estate. In 2004, Paul traded his hockey jersey for a suit and tie and has since built a real estate empire that is nothing short of Stanley Cup material. Since 2007, the Paul Rushforth Team has ranked as the #1 Residential Real Estate Team in Ottawa and finished 2009 as #1 Keller Williams Team Worldwide. Early in 2011, Paul opened his own real estate company, Paul Rushforth Real Estate, Inc. with no end in sight.

Building a reputable & successful real estate team has allowed Paul to separate himself from the competition with aggressive marketing and advertising strategies that sell homes fast and for more money. Paul's radio show, Open House, the Real Estate & Mortgage Show as well as the Gemini Award nominated network TV show "All For Nothing" are wide reaching and help audiences and people who he normally would be unable to personally help.

16

Negotiating a Win-Win Deal

Michael Lewis
Lewis Real Estate Group
Flower Mound, Texas

ANSWERS FROM EXPERTS ON BUYING A HOME

There is no question that for a buyer, getting a good deal in today's market is as easy as can be. Since the real estate market started to take a tumble, the 21st century home buyer has leverage to the hilt. With the power of the internet and the media, the buyer has powerful bargaining tools that should not be underestimated. When preparing to negotiate with a seller, the buyer should use these powerful bargaining tools to their advantage. Of course, most home buyers and home sellers want to arrive at a win-win agreement, but that's not to say either side would regret getting a bigger "win" than the other. To be successful in negotiation, a buyer needs to rely on more than just luck or natural talent.

The first step in getting a deal is finding an agent that will help the buyer achieve their goals—not an agent who just wants to get a deal done. When the buyer begins looking for an agent, they should shop for an agent in the same way that they would shop for a good attorney, accountant, mechanic, plumber, doctor, financial advisor, or other professional. Referrals from friends and family are the first and best place to begin the search, but the internet is also a great source.

With the internet, the buyer has more information at their fingertips than buyers from the past, and has every reason to use this resource to their advantage. For example, if an agent has lots of information on their website and seems genuinely concerned about informing home buyers, that agent is probably a better choice than one whose website lacks useful information.

When interviewing agents for the job, the buyer wants someone who will be concerned with their interests. A good agent will also be sharp enough to ask the buyer questions, including questions about their financial situation. By asking these questions, an agent can make a determination about how they can best represent the buyer's interests. Last, the buyer needs an agent who is bold enough to talk straight, rather than one who will only tell the buyer what they want to hear. When a buyer has found an agent who meets these criteria, they have found the right one.

When the buyer has laid eyes on a desirable property, they must first leave their emotions at the door. A buyer who starts off trying to negotiate with emotions will lose every time. First, a buyer needs to look at how long a home has been on the market, and then find out if there have been any price reductions on the home. Second, the buyer needs to look at the tax value of the home by consulting the tax records. A real estate agent can help in this process, as they can find out if there are any previous offers on the home that have fallen through, or if the seller is currently negotiating another offer.

When the buyer is ready to put pen to paper, the next step is to determine the offer price. When preparing an offer to purchase a home, the buyer already knows the seller's asking price. The question, though, is what price to offer, and how to go about coming up with that figure. Determining the offer price can be summed up in an easy, three-step process.

The first step in determining the offer price is to look at the recent sales of similar homes in the Multiple Listing Service

(MLS), provided by an agent. These are called "comparable sales," and they are very important to look at, being recent sales of homes in the area that compare closely to the one in question. Specifically, the buyer will want to compare prices of homes that are similar in square footage, number of bedrooms and bathrooms, garage space, lot size, and type of construction.

The second step is to look at the most easily accessible source of information on comparable sales: the public records. When someone buys a home, the property is deeded from the seller to the buyer. In most circumstances, this deed is recorded at the local county recorder's office. This makes it easy to use the public record as a source of data for comparable sale information.

The third step is looking at the pending sales in the neighborhood. Pending sales are those homes that have gone under contract in the last thirty days. Of course, the most valuable information would be the most current. A sale last week has more validity to a buyer trying to determine a purchase price than a sale from six months ago. The problem is that there is no actual record of the sales price until the transaction is completed. Looking at this data shows if another buyer has an offer on a home, and shows what the last list price was for the home.

To ensure that the buyer's offer is razor sharp, the buyer should make sure to send their pre-approval letter with the offer to show the seller that they are a serious buyer. This is a good tool to get the seller to come down a little bit more. Also, the buyer should send an informal letter with the offer, a letter that talks about themselves and their family, explains why they want the home, and details why it would be good for them. This shows the seller that they are dealing with a real person with real concerns, and that it is not somebody just trying to get them to come down on price for no reason.

The buyer should choose a 30 to 45 day closing, so the seller also can see that they mean business and want the home fast. The buyer should ask the seller for a quick response time, so as not to be waiting more than 48 hours for an answer. Finally, the buyer needs to respect the priorities of the other party. Knowledge about what is most important to the person on the other side of the negotiating table can help avoid conflicts on hot or sensitive issues.

The last step is compromise. A compromise between buyer and seller on a few issues occurs so that a win-win deal can be put together. "Win-win," however, doesn't mean that both the buyer and the seller will get everything they want. It means both sides will win some and give some but, at the end of the day, both sides go home happy. Using these tips will get the buyer to the closing table and beyond—every time, on time. A win-win deal is a perfect deal.

About The Author

Michael Lewis

Lewis Real Estate Group
3624 Long Prairie #100
Flower Mound, TX 75022

(972) 691-7005

michael@michaellewisteam.com

www.michaellewisteam.com

Michael Lewis has been successfully selling real estate in the Dallas/Fort Worth metroplex since early 2001 and is consistently recognized by the Texas Real Estate Commission Dallas/Fort Worth metroplex as being in the top 1% of all real estate agents in Texas.

Michael Lewis brings extensive knowledge and experience to his real estate career gained from previously owning several prosperous companies. A thriving entrepreneur, Michael currently owns and operates Lewis Real Estate Group. He believes and works with a servant's mentality teaching in his local real estate community while becoming a leader in helping other agents achieve success.

Michael is a graduate of North Central Texas College. His practice is deeply rooted in educating buyers and sellers and walking with them step-by-step to ensure their success in achieving their dreams of home ownership.

17

Finding Favorable Financing

Adrian Petrila
Realty Direct
Naples, Florida

Whether buying a first home, or upgrading to a larger home, it is vital that home buyers have good credit to ensure favorable financing terms. Otherwise, home buyers may find that they pay thousands more, even tens of thousands more, in interest costs. So, how does one maintain good credit and how does this help when it comes to mortgage financing? This chapter will outline some of the factors that are important for home-buyers seeking favorable financing.

Understanding Credit Scores

It is important that those who are thinking about buying a home understand how credit scores work, as well as how these scores affect their financing. By knowing what improves credit scores, as well as what negatively affects credit scores, potential home owners can change their spending habits to more positively influence their credit.

Credit scores range from 300 to 850 points on the FICO scale. According to MSN Money, the average credit score in the United States is 720, and only 13% of the population can boast a score of over 800. A higher credit score is better, with a score over 740 considered ideal for acquiring good financing terms. However, a score from 695 to 740 is still fairly good.

If a potential home buyer's score is less than 695, then it may be advisable for them to spend a few months trying to improve their credit score before applying for home financing. The effort spent improving credit score can translate into huge savings on home financing.

How Credit Scores Affect Financing

Many home buyers make the mistake of thinking that their credit scores won't have a large affect on their home financing. These buyers are usually unpleasantly surprised to find that they will be paying much more in interest charges due to their less-than-favorable credit scores. Here is an example:

Two individuals are considering the purchase of a $200,000 home in Seattle, WA, with both individuals having a 5% down payment and similar job and financial histories. Person A has a credit score of 705, while Person B has a better credit score of over 740. Person A can secure an annual percentage rate (APR) of 4.653% (as of May, 2011), while person B is offered 4.451%.

Now, if either individual had a credit score from 660 to 679, the best rate they could secure would be 5.205%. While it may not sound like there is much difference between these rates, over the life of a 30-year term, the amount paid on the $190,000 loan equates to the following:

Table 17-1

Interest Rate	Total Interest Paid (30 Years)	Difference From Base Rate
4.451%	$154,584.16	
4.653%	$162,814.79	$8,230.63
5.205%	$185,803.14	$31,218.98

Table 17-1 clearly shows how much it pays to keep a good credit score, as, in the above example, a bad credit score results in $31,000 more in interest charges. These charges can climb even higher if banks assign penalty points to a mortgage. Higher financing rates also mean higher mortgage payments, which may make it harder for individuals to secure financing on the home they want, or may mean they have to sacrifice other expenditures to make their monthly payments.

Raising Credit Scores

Having a good credit score can ensure that the financing rates offered by mortgage brokers and banks are as low as possible, which can reduce mortgage payments and minimize interest costs. Before considering purchasing a home, it is a good idea to take the following steps:

1) Check Scores

The first step to improving a credit score is to ensure that there are no errors on the report. Errors can occur for a number of reasons, such as when an account is attributed to an individual that it doesn't actually belong to, when late payments are recorded when payments were actually sent on time, or when old information (over 7 years) is not removed from the report. If an error is detected, the home buyer can contact the accounting department of the company who made the error and inquire about correction. It can take up to 30 days for errors to be corrected, occasionally longer, so home buyers are advised to request error correction well in advance of applying for a loan.

2) Get a Card and Use It

While some people may boast of "owing nothing," this can in fact have a negative effect on their credit score. Good credit scores are awarded when applicants for financing can show that they are able to take on debt, and then pay it off in a reasonable amount of time.

Those looking to improve credit scores should start by ensuring that they have at least one major credit card (such as American Express, Visa, Master Card, or Discover Card), and that they regularly use the card, while making payments at the end of the month. By showing that they can accumulate debt and pay it off, card holders are helping to improve their credit scores.

3) Never Miss Payments

Even a single missed payment can affect credit scores, so it is a good idea for anyone wishing to keep or improve on their credit score to set up automatic payments. This ensures that monthly payments are made on time, with no exceptions.

4) Spread Debt Out

Credit scores are greatly affected by how much of a credit card's limit is used up. For example, if a single card carries a 50% debt load, while the card holder's other card has no balance the card holder will be penalized with lower credit scores for carrying high debt on the one card. A good rule of thumb is to keep each credit card's debt load to less than 25% (or even 10%), even if this means spreading the debt out over several cards.

5) Apply for an Installment Loan

If a potential home buyer is looking to improve their credit score, but is carrying a high credit card debt ratio, then an installment loan may be a wise choice. By moving debt off credit cards and to another type of loan, credit scores should improve over a relatively short period of time.

6) Keep Accounts Open

Although card holders may be tempted to close some of their credit card accounts in order to consolidate bills and payments, as far as credit scores are concerned, this is not a wise idea. Credit scores are based on long-term data, and closing an account may have a negative effect on scores. It is also a good idea to break out old cards once in a while for a purchase so they keep reporting.

7) Keep Limits As-Is

Whether a card holder needs a $15,000 limit or not, it is better to keep credit limits on the high side, since part of a credit score is based on how much of a credit card's limit is being used. It is better to have a $1,500 balance that equals 10% of a card's limit than the same (or even a lesser) balance that equals 75% of a card's limit.

8) Avoiding Financing Penalties

While credit scores are one of the main tools that finance companies use to determine the mortgage applicant's interest rate, it is not the only thing they consider. Other factors, such as the size of the down payment, the debt-to-income ratio, money-saving history, job history, and recent loans will impact finance rates.

CHAPTER 17 – FINDING FAVORABLE FINANCING

It is recommended that home buyers wishing to secure a good finance rate refrain from making any significant financial changes prior to closing on a home, including taking out personal or automobile loans and changing jobs. Banks are looking for stability, great payment and saving history, as well as good credit scores. By ensuring that they have all of these, home buyers can secure the best finance rates possible.

About The Author

Adrian Petrila

Realty Direct
4500 Executive Drive #330
Naples, FL 34119

(239) 598-9393

apetrila@adrianpetrila.com

www.adrianpetrila.info

Adrian Petrila started his real estate career in 2002 and has been involved in residential sales, new home construction, vacant land, broker price opinions, and distressed sale properties. His career successes include receiving Craig Proctor's Quantum Leap Award, $1M GCI Award, completing over 15,000 broker valuations, selling 150-200 homes per year, and being the #1 real estate agent (out of more than 4,000 agents) in Naples, FL, from 2008-2011 by total homes sold.

After several years as an individual agent, Adrian began building his real estate team in 2006. In 2008, he opened his own brokerage. Today he is the owner of three Realty Direct franchise offices in southwest Florida with over 150 agents. He is also the founder and CEO of BPOGenius.com, a software company servicing real estate agents in the valuation industry.

Adrian is an active member of the National Association of REO Brokers (NRBA), Diamond Mastermind Group, and REO4Kids. He also supports children's charities including Make-A-Wish Foundation, Boys and Girls Club of America and others.

18

Preparing for Property Taxes

Igor Krasnoperov
Rising Star Realty
Mohegan Lake, New York

ANSWERS FROM EXPERTS ON BUYING A HOME

Real estate taxes are a very important topic to home buyers. Most homeowners expect that their property taxes will increase, especially with municipal budgets growing each year. You may not be aware that in some cases, your taxes actually decrease after a home purchase. Buyers need to understand what they can do to make sure that they do not overpay on property taxes.

How much will a home owner have to pay in real property taxes? Property taxes depend upon the town, city, and school budgets in the local municipality. When a local budget is approved, it is spread out among all property owners based upon the assessed value of each property. Each property owner pays no more and no less than what is required to fully fund the budget.

The millage rate (also known as the tax rate) is a figure applied to the assessed value of a property to calculate the property tax liability. One "mill" equals a single dollar of tax on every thousand dollars of taxable value. Calculating the property tax is a matter of multiplying the assessed value of the property by the mill rate and dividing it by 1,000. For example, a property with an assessed value of $50,000, located in a municipality with a mill rate of 20 would have a property tax bill of $1,000 per year.

What makes these details so important to know? They can have adverse financial consequences! The buyer who does their research upfront can save thousands of dollars by preventing themselves from buying a home with taxes that exceed their budget.

CHAPTER 18 - PREPARING FOR PROPERTY TAXES

Real estate agents should be familiar with the assessment rules and guidelines. A buyer should ask a prospective agent general questions about taxes and assessments before hiring one — the answers to these questions will demonstrate the agent's level of knowledge and experience.

Next, the buyer should consider how the assessed value of a property is determined. Over the last few years, real estate values have been rapidly declining all over the country — an unfortunate reality. In many American towns, declines in value of over 20% from their peak are not unusual. With home values declining, many homeowners think that their tax bills will decline as well. But this is just not true.

This is a misconception born from the idea that fair market value and assessed value are the same, but they are not. While fair market value is defined as the price that a willing buyer will pay, the assessed value is usually a price tag set by a municipality to collect a certain amount in taxes.

While many municipalities attempt to adjust their assessed values based on the performance of the real estate market, in most cases, the assessed value is not accurate. The responsibility of the tax assessor is to determine the assessed value of a property. First, the assessor does not increase a property owner's taxes. Next, keeping values up-to-date each year does not necessarily mean that taxes will remain the same. Some properties experience a change in assessed value, as relative market values can go up or down.

For residential properties, the assessor uses similar properties sold in the same neighborhoods to determine a value, while giving consideration to other factors (such as amenities) that may affect the value. At the end of the day, it is up to the home owner to decide whether or not they agree with this assessment.

For example, if a home's assessed value is $350,000 and annual taxes are $7,000, and if the actual market value of the home is only $280,000, this could potentially lead to a decrease in taxes. But what if the market value is higher than the assessed value? Let's say the market value is $420,000. The likely result is an increase in taxes, but many factors can contribute to the decision, including changes in the town or school budget. To ensure that you are buying a property you can afford, you need to do your homework <u>before</u> the purchase, not after.

There is a presumption under the law that the assessment made by the assessor is correct, and the burden of proof lies with the homeowner to challenge this presumption. So, what should a home owner do if they believe that they are not being taxed fairly? In most communities, the property owner can meet informally with the tax assessor about the assessment.

If, after doing so, the home owner still feels that they have been over-assessed, they should go to their local tax assessor's office and file for a grievance, making sure they file their application for grievance before the due date of the actual bill. In filing for a grievance, the home owner needs to prove their property's fair market value. The following scenario is commonly seen in these grievance cases:

If the home was recently purchased, the HUD-1 closing statement will be needed. A homeowner may think that their local town has a record of the recent sale and will base their assessed value on the sale price, but they may not. It is up to the home owner to provide this information. This type of grievance case is usually easily settled through an informal meeting with the assessor.

As long as the sale wasn't forced (as in a divorce or relocation) and took place between two formerly unknown parties (not between relatives or friends), the assessor will probably accept the sale price as a representation of the home's fair market value. If a home was not recently sold, fair market value can be determined by reviewing sales of at least three comparable properties. The comparable sales should include characteristics similar to the home in question, such as lot size, square footage, home style, age, and location.

For example, a new three-bedroom Cape Cod-style house may be on the same street as an older three-bedroom Ranch-style house, but the two may have been sold for very different prices. The assessor will establish a time frame for the "recent sales" on which comparable sales can be based, and will reject comparisons that don't fall within that time frame.

Some home owners, in this situation will hire an appraiser in the hope that the assessor will look more favorably on the appraiser's opinion. If they are right, they will be able to offset the appraiser's fee with their tax savings. Home owners also have the option of using a company that specializes in tax grievances.

Home owners should also know that even if their assessed value is correct, they may still be paying more in taxes that they should. A home owner might determine that the assessment was based on market value, but find that the rest of the community is assessed at a lower percentage value. State laws require that assessments be made at a uniform percentage of value, so a home owner can claim unequal assessment if they believe that other properties have been assessed at a lower percentage.

For example, if the home owner can prove that the market value of their property is $200,000, and that they received an assessment of $175,000, then it can be shown that they were assessed at 87.5% of market value. If they can also prove that all other properties have, on average, been assessed at only 50% of market value, the home owner can make a claim to get the assessment reduced to $100,000. In most cases, these issues can be resolved through an informal meeting with the assessor.

If the home owner feels that the assessor made an improper ruling on the grievance request, they can appeal the decision. Each state has a different appeal process, but in most cases the appeal must be made within thirty days of when the final assessment is filed. A private attorney is recommended if you opt for this route, as it will be the last chance to change the decision until the next tax year. Each year brings a new tax assessment and a new opportunity to review the value.

Tax exemptions are another way for homeowners to save on their taxes. There are many different tax exemptions for which home owners can apply and there is no cost associated with getting an exemption. Potentially, a home owner could be exempt from all or part of their property tax obligations, as long as the home owner can meet the various requirements. Some of the exemptions include:

Basic Exemption—offers savings on the school property taxes. This exemption is available for owner-occupied primary residences if the household income falls within a specific range, regardless of age. This is not available in every state.

Senior Citizen Exemption—available to senior citizens (aged 65 or older) who are home owners and have an income within a specific range. If the property is owned by a married couple, only one of them must be 65 or older to qualify for this exemption.

Veterans Exemption—available to individuals who have served in the armed forces.

Volunteer Exemption—available to individuals who participate in volunteer programs, such as fire and ambulance departments.

Disability and Limited Income Exemptions—available to citizens with disabilities or on a limited income.

163

A complete list of local property tax exemptions in the area, along with the relevant application forms and eligibility criteria, can be obtained through the local tax assessor's office.

Hopefully you now understand how important it is for a home owner to be prepared and educated in order to deal with the tax liabilities that can arise through property ownership. While the market value of a home may make it appear to be a good deal, the taxes of the local area may put the actual price of owning that home into a much higher range. Home buyers need to do their homework on the local taxes. Skipping this step could undermine your negotiating power against other buyers who have done their homework.

About The Author

Igor Krasnoperov

Rising Star Realty
1750 East Main St
Mohegan Lake, NY 10547

(914) 243-4885

igor@mysellingsystem.com

www.mysellingsystem.com

Igor Krasnoperov has worked in real estate in the Hudson Valley region of New York since 2001. From 2003 to 2010, Igor was an Associate Broker with Re/Max Classic Realty, where he was recognized with the Re/Max Network's "Hall of Fame" award. In 2009, Igor was named Top RE/MAX Agent in the Hudson Valley region, and the number two agent in New York State, in number of transactions and gross commission income. Igor has also received numerous Diamond Awards (the highest level of recognition) from the local Board.

In 2010, Igor opened Rising Star Realty & Property Management, Inc, his own brokerage. Igor and his team recognize that their clients are their best marketing source.

Continuing education is a very important part of Igor's business philosophy. He has been a member of The Craig Proctor Real Estate Coaching Program since 2003, and has attended numerous conferences and courses to stay on top of the ever-changing real estate laws, marketing approaches, and technology trends.

SUMMARY

We hope the information contained in this book has helped to educate you about the home-buying process and has given you a better idea of questions to ask potential real estate agents before you hire them.

Purchasing a home is the single largest financial investment most people will make during their lifetime. It is important to find an experienced and ethical real estate agent to assist you. If you don't live in a market area serviced by an author of this book, please contact one of us so we can recommend someone in your area who is qualified to help you find your dream home.

We've spent many years in real estate coaching with Craig Proctor, who became the number one selling RE/MAX agent in the world at the age of 26 and remained in the top ten for *sixteen years* until retiring in 2009. Craig's Quantum Leap coaching program is the most expensive real estate education in North America. It provides the agents who invest in themselves with the tools, knowledge, and experience to succeed in any market!

Why would you hire anyone who offers less? Our experience at offer preparation, skillful negotiation, and creative financing strategies can literally save you tens of thousands of dollars. Find us! It will be worth the effort!

Happy Home Buying!

CPSIA information can be obtained at www.ICGtesting.com
Printed in the USA
BVOW071814171211

278627BV00002B/4/P